MBI Publishing Company

JAGUAR

John Heilig

First published in 1997 by MBI Publishing Company, 729 Prospect Avenue, PO Box 1, Osceola, WI 54020-0001 USA

MBI Publishing Company books are also available at discounts in bulk quantity for industrial or sales-promotional use. For details write to Special Sales Manager Motorbooks International Wholesalers & Distributors, 729 Prospect Avenue, PO Box 1, Osceola, WI 54020-0001 USA.

Edited by Anne McKenna
Designed by Katie Finney

Library of Congress Cataloging-in-Publication Data
Heilig, John.
    Jaguar/ John Heilig.
       p. cm.—(Enthusiast color series)
    Includes index.
    ISBN 0-7603-0352-5 (pbk. : alk. paper)
    1. Jaguar automobile—History. I. Title. II. Series.
TL215.J3H45   1997
629.222'2--dc21   97-19419

On the front cover: The 1953 XK120M had an improved 3.4-liter XK engine that delivered 190 horsepower. The "M" in the model name was for Modified.

On the back cover: In 1996, Jaguar introduced its first all-new sports car in 30 years, the XK8. The Roadster version exhibits clean aerodynamic lines, combined with touches reminiscent of the E-type—wide oval grille, long nose and short tail.

On the frontis: Although safety legislation of the 1980s dictated that "unsafe" ornamentation should be removed to prevent injury, the infamous Jaguar "leaper" hood ornament appears on select Jaguar sedans of the 1990s.

On the title page: The 1996 XJS was only offered as a convertible and only with the 6.0-liter V-12 engine. This was the last full year of production for the XJS.

Printed in China

CONTENTS

Acknowledgments

William Lyons was a genius. He had the foresight to create a product—initially assembling that product out of readily available components—that the public fell in love with and bought. With the profits gained from these simple products, he developed more complex products and established an automobile company that has persisted for over 70 years.

That company, of course, is Jaguar. And while Lyons began by building motorcycle sidecars with his neighbor, William Walmsley, the cars he created toward the end of his life were exotic sports cars and luxury sedans that had no equal in the world.

Like most youths of the 1950s, I loved the legend of Jaguar. I had an MG budget, but a Jaguar was always the goal. Eventually, I was able to buy an aged 3.4 sedan (for $300) that at least brought me some of the thrill of owning the sports cars. But despite the fact that the 3.4 appeared to have been built with quarter-inch-thick steel in the fenders, the transmission was fragile and broke. I wasn't up to attempting the repairs or restoration, so I traded it in on a more practical economy car.

Today, the products of Jaguar are luxury sedans and one of the best sports cars in the world, the XK8. Things haven't changed much over the last 45 years. In 1989, Ford stepped in and rescued what is one of the last bastions of a once-thriving British automobile industry. The company that has survived after the Ford take-over is not emasculated, as many feared. It is, instead, stronger than ever and retains a level of independence that permits it to continue to develop its sedans and sports cars with a distinctly British flavor.

Many people helped in this project, most particularly Chris Gennone of Communication Dynamics International, who was its catalyst and who provided support, fact-checking and editorial assistance. Another source of great moral, editorial and photographic support was Len Alcaro of Jaguar Cars North America, who checked the manuscript and also made cars available to photograph.

Special thanks must be given to Don Vorderman, who graciously allowed me to use portions of his unpublished work on Bill Lyons. Also, thanks to Margaret Harrison for her photographs and to the Automobile Quarterly Photo and Research Library for supplying photographs when the original source dried up.

Car owners whose vehicles are in here include the late Jim Spooner, and Les Jackson, Jaguar Cars of North America,

As with anything I do, this couldn't have been completed without the love and support of my wife, Florence, our three daughters, Susan, Sharon and Laura, and their honeys. Well, it could have been completed, but it wouldn't have been worth it.

The Prewar Years

Chapter One

There would never have been a Jaguar car if there had never been a William Lyons. And Lyons might never have begun his life's work if there had not been a William Walmsley. Lyons, who was eventually to be knighted for his work with Jaguar, was designer, engineer, visionary and activist for Jaguar and the companies that would precede it. When he retired in 1972, the company lost its driving force and spirit, and lost its way for a couple of years. That it has been able to revive itself in the past 25 years is a credit to the organization that Lyons created and the men who worked so hard to save it, particularly John Egan, who would also be knighted.

1932 SS1 FIXED HEAD COUPE
The SS1 was the first full automobile built by William Lyons and William Walmsley. Introduced in October 1931, the SS1 had a modified 6-cylinder Standard chassis supplied by John Black of the Standard Motor Company. The underslung frame provided for a low body. Lyons wanted a body that was even lower than the production car, but Walmsley signed off on the slightly higher version when Lyons was in the hospital with appendicitis.

Don Vorderman, former editor of *Automobile Quarterly*, said of Lyons: "Had he done nothing else but serve as chief stylist at Jaguar, had he done nothing more than supervise the development of the SS100, or the XK120, or the prewar or postwar saloons, his place in the pantheon of automotive design would be secure. The remarkable fact is that he did all of these cars and a dozen or so more while simultaneously directing the operations of a major automobile company.

"A varied assortment of talents were present, all functioning smoothly and independently within him. Lyons' exquisite sense of design was merely one, but perhaps the most evident of his gifts. He also oversaw the engineering and advertising departments. He orchestrated their racing programs. He was a diplomat, too, having to deal with unions and successive governments that were all too often inclined to interfere with this or that aspect of his business.

"Of course he didn't create these legendary designs entirely on his own. There were a number

William Lyons' love of motorcycles is what led to the formation of Jaguar Cars. Lyons met William Walmsley, who had established a small factory to build motorcycle sidecars in the garage behind his home. Lyons bought a sidecar from Walmsley, and the two decided to go into business together to make sidecars. They grew the business to include building of custom bodies for Austin chassis, and eventually began designing their own cars on Standard chassis. From these Standard Swallows the Jaguar was born.

of talented people to assist him, most notably Malcolm Sayer, but while he was there, Bill Lyons had the first and last word on the design of every car Jaguar built." But we're getting ahead of ourselves.

William Lyons was born September 4, 1901, in the village of Blackpool. His father was an Irish musician who visited Blackpool one year as a member of an orchestra that was hired for holiday entertainment. Lyons Sr. never returned home, because he met and fell in love with a local girl,

Minnie. They were married and William Sr. opened a music store and sold pianos. When William Jr. was born, his father's music business was well-established.

As a youth, Lyons apprenticed at Crossley Motors Ltd. When he was 18, he began working for Brown and Mallalieu, a local car dealer, as a junior salesman.

Like most youths of the era, Lyons liked motorcycles. England had not yet been blessed with a "people's car" like the Model T Ford, so young dandies from middle-class families would buy motorcycles and attach sidecars as basic transportation.

Lyons first met William Walmsley when Walmsley's family moved into the same Blackpool neighborhood. Walmsley had been developing a small business in the family garage building sidecars for motorcycles. Lyons, who had owned an early Harley-Davidson, discovered Walmsley's business and bought a sidecar. The two eventually decided to join forces in 1922, but Lyons was still under the legal age of 21 required to acquire loans from banks. They had to wait until September 4, 1922, before founding the Swallow Sidecar Company with £1000 (around $5,000). The factory was at 7-9 Bloomfield Rd., in Blackpool.

Swallow Sidecars built as many as 10 zeppelin-shaped sidecars a week, fitted to chassis built by Montgomery's of Coventry. The most expensive chassis they sold cost £30.

In 1924, the same year Lyons married Greta Brown, Tourist Trophy entrants with Swallow sidecars finished second, third, and fourth in the annual motorcycle race on the Isle of Man.

Two years later, the company moved to larger premises in Cocker Street. It changed its name to the Swallow Sidecar & Coach Building Company because they had begun offering repairs to auto-

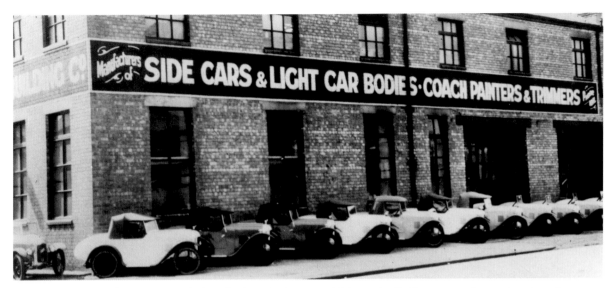

The original Swallow factory was in Blackpool, where "side cars and light car bodies" were manufactured, and coaches were painted and trimmed. The small Austin Swallows are lined up in front of the factory, showing their trim bodies that attracted someone who wanted the economy of an Austin Seven but not its utilitarian looks.

mobile bodies. This was all in preparation for a new business that would commence in January 1927, but which began with the introduction of the Austin Seven in 1922.

The Austin Seven was a genuine British car for the mass market, but it also proved to be a very good chassis on which to build custom bodies. Called the Seven because of its taxable horsepower, the little Austin was simple in design and execution. Lyons knew that he could buy a chassis for little money and could build a custom-bodied car for a reasonable asking price. The factory cars were also plain and wouldn't provide any competition for a custom design.

Lyons and Walmsley bought an Austin Seven chassis in 1927 for £100 and built their first car, designed by Lyons. It was a two-seater sports model with a top that was hinged at the rear. When this application proved to be awkward in the wind, the hinging was moved to the front for production models. Success of the Austin Swallow

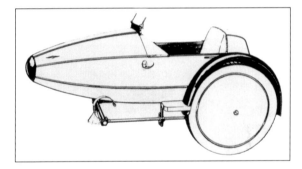

The Swallow sidecars were aluminum, torpedo-shaped and relatively aerodynamic. They provided the youth of the 1920s with a means of transporting themselves and a companion, since there was no equivalent of the inexpensive Model T Ford in England at the time. Later, the Austin Seven would serve that purpose, so Lyons was fortunate that he was born at the right time.

was assured when Henley's of London, a large Austin dealer, ordered 500 cars.

In mid-1928, a four-door Swallow sedan joined the lineup, also built on an Austin Seven chassis. Once again, the company changed its name, to the Swallow Coachbuilding Company,

1935 SS1 AIRLINE SALOON
Before they were Jaguars, William Lyons built the SS1, which was the first car totally designed by the Swallow Coachbuilding Company, predecessor to Jaguar. The SS1 was built on a modified 6-cylinder Standard chassis, supplied to Lyons and William Walmsley for this purpose. With a low-slung chassis and the engine set back 7 inches from where it was in the Standard, stylish bodies were possible. This body is an Airline Saloon, or sedan. Airline designs were the fastbacks of the 1930s, and similar products from companies such as MG remain stylish to today. *Margaret Harrison*

indicating future intent. Swallow still built motor-cycle sidecars, and would through World War II, but automobiles would play a larger and larger role in the company's affairs.

"The (Swallow) bodies were attractive," wrote Ken Purdy. "They ran to split windshields, external sun visors, wire wheels, and good options in two-tone paint jobs—but the running gear under them was never up to the performance the coachwork seemed to promise."

In November 1928, Swallow moved to Coventry, England, in the center of the British automobile industry. It was the equivalent of a new American automobile manufacturer moving its operations to Detroit. The building was an old artillery shell-filling factory.

Swallow built cars on chassis supplied by Austin, Wolseley, Morris, Swift, Standard and the Fiat 509. Eventually, designs on the Morris chassis were abandoned when Morris began building a more sporty version of its own cars and called it MG.

In May 1931, John Black, managing director of the Standard Motor Company, agreed to sell a modified 6-cylinder Standard chassis to Swallow for the creation of Swallow's first total design, the SS1. Standard agreed to modify the

1936 SS1 AIRLINE DROPHEAD COUPE

SS Cars Ltd. built several body variations on the SS1 chassis. This Drophead Coupe is what is referred to in the United States as a convertible, with a removable top. Some drophead coupes had landau irons framing the C-pillar area of the top, but in the case of the SS1, the top is simpler. The Airline coupes were powered by 2,143 and 2,663 side valve 6-cylinder engines that were derived from the Standard 16 and Standard 20, respectively. *Margaret Harrison*

1936 SS1 AIRLINE SALOON

This SS1 Airline Saloon has a different rear treatment than the 1935 SS1 Airline Saloon. The rear styling is more conventional, with a square addition to the body for the trunk. *Margaret Harrison*

1934 SS1
By the time the 1934 SS1 was produced, the wheelbase had been extended 7 inches. The company had gone public in 1933, and co-founder William Walmsley had left. Lyons was in full control now, and the roofline of the 1934 SS1 reflected his taste more.

chassis by adding 3 inches to the wheelbase and stuffing in a higher axle ratio for more top speed—but of course, less acceleration. The frame was underslung and the engine was set back 7 inches. The first SS1 cars were introduced in October 1931 at the London Motor Show, along with the SS2, which was essentially an SS1 with a 30-inch shorter chassis. Incidentally, nobody is certain as to the exact meaning of "SS," since it was never well-defined. It could have stood for "Swallow Sports," "Standard Swallow," or "Swallow Side-car," but neither Lyons nor Walmsley ever revealed what they were thinking.

Vorderman, an owner of numerous Jaguars, wrote, "It was with the announcement of the SS1 late in 1931, based on still another manufacturer's running gear, that Lyons burst out of obscurity to become one of the most respected figures in the British automobile business, a position he would occupy with dignity and grace for the rest of his life."

"The SS1 of 1932 knocked the British industry on its collective ear," Vorderman continued, "offering what journalists began calling 'The car with the 1,000 pound look'—that's nearly the price of a contemporary Bentley chassis—but it cost only £310. It was about that time that people began asking each other the question that would follow Jaguars around for years to come, 'How can they do it for the money?' The truth is that there was a great deal of profit to be made in the building and selling of coachbuilt motorcars in those days. In creating the SS1, Lyons had simply selected a proven, inexpensive chassis from the Standard Motor Company, had it slightly modified to his own specifications and then set up a production line to mass produce hand-built bodies for it, hundreds at a time. Simple."

The SS1 was known primarily for its style, rather than its performance. Both the coupe and two-door sedan had long hoods, flowing fenders, wire wheels and low rooflines. Actually, Lyons wanted a roofline that was even lower than the one that appeared on the cars, but Walmsley signed off on a more practical version when Lyons was in the hospital with appendicitis.

Based on the Standard 16 horsepower chassis, it was officially known as the SS Sixteen. Later, a larger 20 horsepower engine was also offered.

In 1933, the company's name was changed again, to SS Cars Ltd. William Lyons was named Chairman and Managing Director. In 1934, he proposed going public with the company. William Walmsley didn't share Lyons' ambition, and resigned amicably, turning total control of SS Cars over to Lyons. Walmsley was a practical engineer who was as happy tinkering with his model railroad trains as he was with cars.

The 1933 version of the SS1 had a 7-inch longer wheelbase and an underslung chassis, which gave a lower seating position and the lower roofline that Lyons had originally wanted.

The shorter SS2 that appeared at the same time as the SS1 was known as the "little brother" to the bigger car. The car was powered by 9, 10 and 12 horsepower Standard engines. The SS2 retained some of the panache of the bigger car, albeit in a more compact fashion.

Lyons introduced his first sports model, the SS90, early in 1935. It was soon followed by the more powerful SS100. Between the introductions, Lyons was also hard at work thinking of a new name for the cars. One of the names he considered was "Sunbeam," but the Rootes organization had secured the rights to that name. "Jaguar" was eventually chosen. But first, Lyons had to obtain permission from Armstrong-Siddely, another Coventry firm that had a tradition of giving big cat names to their airplane engines—Cougar, Cheetah and Lynx, for example.

The first car to carry that name, SS Jaguar, was a sedan version of the SS90 with wire wheels. A Tourer version of the car was also introduced in 1935. In September, the SS Jaguar 100 was advertised as "an entirely new SS for 1936." Priced at £385 ($1,900), and available in 1½ (1608cc) and 2½ (2662cc) liter versions, it generated more than 100 horsepower with the larger engine.

The extra power was derived from a head design by Harry Weslake, who was England's greatest expert on cylinder head design and who was working as a consultant to Lyons. His overhead valve head for the Standard six increased the power of the 2.6-liter engine from 70 to 100 horsepower. Working for Jaguar as chief engineer was William Heynes, who joined the company in 1935.

British writer John Stanford, in *The Sports Car*, said in 1962 of the first cars to bear the Jaguar name: "The introduction . . . of the first Jaguar series saw the beginnings of a really well-merited rise to spectacular success. Like the modern Jaguars, they were the work of William M. Heynes; and had very robust pushrod o.h.v. engines, well-chosen gear ratios, and rigid, rather stiffly sprung chassis. From the beginning, an open short-chassis version was available with 2½- or 3½-liter engine, at a very low price. The opulent and slightly flashy

1937 SS100
The SS100, introduced in 1935, was the first sport car introduced by Swallow. At this time, William Lyons was thinking of a new name for his company. Later versions of the SS100 would reflect that name—Jaguar. The SS100 was available in 1 1/2- and 2 1/2-liter versions, with the latter generating more than 100 horsepower. An SS100 could go 100 miles per hour, and the car was victorious in many races, hillclimbs and rallies.

lines, with their rakish swept wings and exaggerated long bonnets, have dated somewhat to modern eyes; and with the engine well forward in the very short chassis, handling was apt to leave some room for improvement. None the less, performance was available in full measure, both versions having top speeds closely approaching 100 miles per hour with considerable refinement."

American writer Ken Purdy wrote: "The SS1 and SS2 passenger cars were backed up by sports models—SS90, SS100—because Lyons, whose grasp of the fundamentals has never been less than brilliant, knew that competition effort was vital to sales, particularly in Europe and particularly then. A good SS100 would do 100 miles per hour and the model had notable successes in rallies, hill climbs, and sports car races. An SS100 won the International Alpine Trial of 1936 (and again in 1948) and the 1937 Royal Automobile Club Rally. The car would not only run, it had visual appeal to burn—a happy amalgam of the design points that were the desiderata of the day: big flat-lens headlights, flaring fenders, louvers all over the hood, curved dashboard carrying saucer-sized main instruments, a saddle gas tank hung astern. Only a few SS100s were made and the survivors are all classics." Tommy Wisdom and his wife Elsie (or "Bill") won the 1934 Alpine Trial in a factory-sponsored car.

In 1937, a 3½-liter version of the SS Jaguar 100 was introduced and immediately earned its stripes in competition. Sammy Newsome set the fastest time at the Shelsley Walsh hill climb in a 3½-liter SS100. Tommy Wisdom won the Long Handicap race at Brooklands in the same car.

"The SS100 is certainly one of the best looking sports cars ever built," wrote Don Vorderman. "Its swooping wings, extremely low build, its long, louvered bonnet, excellent cockpit and lavish instrumentation were the perfect expression of the sports car of the 1930s. The fact that it wasn't nearly as fast as it looked and had whimsical mechanical brakes seemed to have little effect on people's enthusiasm for it. A little more than 300 SS100s were made from 1936 into 1940, and according to the Jaguar Register, most of them are still around, arousing lustful thoughts among a new generation of car fanciers and appreciating at a dizzying rate."

For the 1938 model year, SS Jaguar sedans changed from wood frames to all-steel construction. The 3½-liter engine joined the sedan lineup that year as well. In a trend away from sportiness, the spare tire was moved from its location on the fender to under the floor of the trunk.

Purdy: "To give the first SS Jaguar the performance its appearance called for, Lyons had asked the designer Harry Weslake to modify Standard's side-valve engine into an overhead-valve unit and had brought in W.M. Heynes to oversee engineering, the beginning of an enduring association with the company for both men. Heynes was a vice-chairman when he retired, full of honors, in 1969. Like the SS1 that had gone before it, the new SS Jaguar sedan looked more expensive than it was: a poll of dealers at its introduction showed an average price guess of £632 ($3,000), but the sticker was only £385 ($1885). The model was another smash success (it was called the poor man's Bentley, sometimes admiringly, sometimes not), and when everything stopped for World War II in September 1939, the firm was turning out 250 cars a week."

Jaguar's oldest established American dealership opened in 1938. Hugh Weidinger's Hempstead Motors on Long Island in New York became an imported car dealership that year and continues today, despite the death in 1995 of its founder. Hempstead Motors sells Jaguars and Mercedes-Benz today, among others but not in the same showroom.

As the 1930s drew to a close, SS Cars Ltd. was a growing company whose products had developed a strong following in England and had earned recognition in the United States as well. Unfortunately, that growth would be put on hold for six years when Great Britain declared war on Germany on September 3, 1939. SS Cars continued to use its remaining stocks of raw materials to build cars as late as the spring of 1940. In the last full year of car production before switching over to war production.

The
1940s

Chapter Two

During the war, Swallow Sidecars, which was still a subsidiary of SS Cars, made more than 10,000 sidecars for British army motorcycles. In addition, the company built 50,000 trailers for the war effort in three different weight classes. Before hostilities began, SS had begun building wing tips for Stirling bombers. Another major effort was the repair and modification of Armstrong Whitworth "Whitley" bombers. Planes would be trucked to the Foleshill plant, where they would be repaired. After repairs were completed, they would be trucked to a local

1948 JAGUAR MARK IV DROPHEAD COUPE
The 1948 "Mark IV" Jaguar sedans and Drophead coupes were postwar versions of the prewar 3 1/2-, 2 1/2- and 1 1/2- liter versions. Although never officially recognized as the Mark IV by the factory, the postwar versions of these cars acquired these names. This Mark IV was powered by a 3 1/2-liter inline 6-cylinder engine that was soon overshadowed by the 6-cylinder XK engine that Jaguar had been developing during the war. This Drophead Coupe was capable of a top speed of 90 miles per hour.

airfield for tests. When the Whitley was taken out of service, SS repaired the "Welington." The company also made components for the Supermarine "Spitfire," Avro "Lancaster," DeHavilland "Mosquito" and Airspeed "Oxford" planes. As the war wound down, SS also built the complete center section of the Gloster "Meteor," which was England's first operational jet-powered fighter.

Toward the end of the war, Walter Hassan, who had joined SS cars from Bentley in 1938, and Claude Bailey designed two lightweight vehicles that were to be parachuted into battle. Called the VA and VB, they were both built with unibody construction and had 4-wheel independent suspensions. The VA was powered by a rear-mounted 1096 JAP motorcycle engine with chain drive. The VB had a Ford 10 horsepower engine and used a 3-speed transmission in a more conventional layout. Because of its rear-mounted engine, the VA had excellent traction, and the front end could be lifted by one man. Neither car pro-

1947 JAGUAR MK IV SEDAN
The first cars Jaguar built after the war were pre-war designs, the Mark IV 3 1/2-liter sedan. This Australian example shows the big headlights typical of pre-war cars, combined with a decidedly vertical architecture, as exemplified by the grille. The sweeping front fenders connect all the way to the rear, offering vestiges of running boards. *Margaret Harrison*

ceeded beyond the prototype stage because the development of transport aircraft went so quickly that it was possible for them to carry heavier loads, and air-drop full-sized Jeeps into battle, rather than specially designed lightweight vehicles.

Because of its location in England's industrial sector, Coventry received a lot of attention from German bombers. The center of the city was the focus of several Luftwaffe blitzkrieg raids. Ken Purdy wrote: ". . . the cathedral in Coventry, England. It had been burned and blown into rubble (during a ten-hour raid) on the night of November 14, 1940, by 500 Luftwaffe bombers in the longest raid England took during the war. Work to rebuild began the

All Jaguar sedans throughout the history of the company have exhibited long hoods, flowing fenders and short rear decks. This 1947 Mark IV 3 1/2-liter Sedan is typical of prewar designs converted to early postwar production. This angle also shows the semaphore turn signals, recessed door handles for both front and rear doors, and the wire wheels so beloved by William Lyons. *Margaret Harrison*

next day, the architect Sir Basil Spence planning the new cathedral on the site of the old, forming some of the standing ruins into it; the cornerstone was laid by the queen sixteen years and a bit later."

As for Jaguar, Browns Lane, 3 miles away from the cathedral, was only badly damaged once. Part of the roof of a newly constructed building on Swallow Road was damaged. Don Vorderman recounts part of Jaguar's legend that has "Lyons and his chief engineer Bill Heynes . . . on air raid watches during World War II, mapping out their postwar plans. At times the obstacles must have seemed nearly insurmountable, with Coventry all but obliterated by the ten-hour air raid. The plan-

1947 JAGUAR MK IV SEDAN
Jaguars, especially the sedans, have featured the "leaper" hood ornament. Safety legislation of the 1980s dictated that such "unsafe" ornamentation should be removed to prevent injury to pedestrians. The leaper remains on select Jaguar sedans of the 1990s. *Margaret Harrison*

Part of the tradition of Jaguar cars has been the wood trim and leather upholstery. Wood-trimmed dash fascias date back to the earliest days of the company, as evidenced in this 1947 Mk IV sedan that was essentially a prewar car rushed into postwar production. This right-hand-drive Australian model also shows some interesting remnants of prewar design, such as the crank to open the bottom of the windshield, and a starter that is separate from the ignition. This car has been modified with the addition of a modern sound system. *Margaret Harrison*

ning continued, and when peace finally came, Jaguar was ready, though unfortunately the rest of the country was not." The company emerged from the war with a larger factory, expanded to increase war production.

One of Lyons' first actions as the war drew to its inevitable conclusion was to change the name of his company once again. SS Cars wasn't a popular name because "SS" had developed a strongly negative reputation during the war, thanks to Hitler's storm troopers (Schutzstaffel). Lyons responded by changing the name to Jaguar Cars Ltd., the name by which it has been known, in one form or another, for over half a century.

His next move was to get out of the sidecar business. Swallow Sidecars was sold, making Jaguar an automobile company once and for all.

Tube Investments bought the Swallow name, and continued producing sidecars until 1956, when it was absorbed by Watsonian, a Birmingham company that also made sidecars and had supplied William Walmsley with his first chassis in 1920. In the mid-1950s, Tube Investments dabbled briefly in the production of the Swallow Doretti sports car.

Lyons' final move was to buy the tooling that built the Standard 2½ and 3½-liter engines, making Jaguar a complete manufacturer. New equipment would be used to build the XK engines that were designed during the war.

The British government decreed that in order for manufacturers to obtain the raw materials necessary to return to production, 50 percent of that production must be exported. Car manufacturers in particular were urged to build vehicles for

Proper sedans of the 1930s carried fully equipped tool sets. In the case of the 1947 Jaguar Mk IV, which was a prewar design rushed into postwar production, the tool kit was included in the trunk and had the tools fitted into the case. Of interest, besides the important tire iron, screwdrivers, wrenches and hammer for wire wheel knock-offs, there is a pump to inflate tires, an oil can, and wire-cutter pliers. *Margaret Harrison*

export, especially to the United States, which was cash rich. Consequently, Jaguar added left-hand-drive cars to the mix late in 1945.

Jaguar was one of the first British manufacturers to return to production and was under way in July 1945. The first cars were modified prewar models. It wasn't until 1948 that a new model was introduced, the Mark V, which was available in sedan or convertible form with a 2½- or 3½-liter engine. This was the first Jaguar with independent front suspension and hydraulic brakes. As Ken Purdy wrote, "It was no ball of fire in performance and it had irritating detail flaws (for one, a heater

that couldn't cope with a brisk autumn day in Connecticut, never mind a Minnesota winter)." People loved the car anyway.

In 1946, Frank Raymond Wilton "Lofty" England joined Jaguar as service manager. He earned his nickname because of his height. England would lend his considerable organizational skills to Jaguar's racing program in the 1950s and would eventually become managing director of the company.

Lyons traveled to the United States for five weeks in 1948, appointing sales and service agents for Jaguar cars. With the government's export policies and Jaguar's potential for sales in the U.S.,

1948 JAGUAR MARK IV DROPHEAD COUPE
Besides the Saloon, or sedan, Jaguar also built Drophead coupe versions of the Mark IV. Still carried over from the prewar version of the car, the Drophead Coupe offered open-air driving. When compared with the SS1 Airlines, the grilles of the Mark IV Drophead Coupes seem taller and more massive. This is true, as the cars themselves were bigger. All were powered by the 2,663 cc 6-cylinder engine, that was now a Jaguar engine, since the factory that built the engines had been taken over from Standard by Jaguar. Note the large headlights, smaller "fog" lights, running lights on the fenders and landau irons on the top. *Margaret Harrison*

establishment of these agents was a smart move. Max Hoffman on the East Coast and Charles Hornburg on the West Coast were named the U.S. distributors. At the time, Jaguar sold 238 cars in the United States in 1948 and 158 in 1949. This was in an imported car market of 15,442 and 11,858, respectively. Incidentally, all the cars imported in those years were either British or French.

All the efforts of the company were not devoted entirely to the war during the struggle. William Heynes, who joined the company in 1935 as chief engineer, and Walter Hassan spent some of their time developing a new engine that would be used in Jaguar cars after the war. They worked on developing these "X" or experimental engines and were up to "XK" when they found a design they felt would work, a double overhead camshaft 6-cylinder of approximately 3.4 liters capacity. The XK engine proved to be the basis of Jaguar engines for more than 30 years after the end of hostilities.

The engine that Heynes and Hassan developed during the war was initially intended for a

This Australian Mark IV Drophead Coupe differs from the black one in that this car has the running lights on the fenders and the rear-view mirrors have been moved from the fender tops to the doors, where they are more practical. Both cars exhibit classic prewar Jaguar styling, with long flowing front fenders sweeping back to the rear fenders, which allows vestiges of running boards on both sides. *Margaret Harrison*

new sedan, which was to be a successor to the Mark V, but the new sedan wasn't ready in time. Therefore, Lyons and crew installed the engine in an aluminum-bodied sports car that was intended to be a stopgap low production vehicle. Since it had the 3.4-liter XK engine and engineers figured the car was capable of a top speed in the neighborhood of 120 miles per hour, it was named "XK120." The car was introduced in October 1948 at the London Motor Show. To confirm the car's potential—and its name—test driver Ron Sutton took an XK120 to the Jabbeke

autoroute in Belgium (a favorite high-speed test track for auto companies) and traveled 132.596 miles per hour over the measured mile. Actor Clark Gable was one of the first buyers of an XK120 after he met Lyons at a cocktail party in Hollywood. In his bylined article in the May 1950 *Road & Track* he claimed to have driven the car 124 miles per hour.

As John Stanford wrote in *The Sports Car*, "That such an engine could be made in large numbers at a relatively low price, and also run, as some have done, for 100,000 miles without over-

1949 JAGUAR MK V

Jaguar introduced the "interim" Mark V sedan when the XK engine that was supposed to go into it was still not ready for production. Hence, the Mark V was powered by the older 3 1/2- and 3 1/2-liter engines that were based on the old prewar Standard engines. What was most significant about the Mark V, though, was its modern chassis, an independent front suspension. The Mark V used 16-inch wheels rather than the 18-inch wheels of its predecessor. Styling was slightly more modern than the Mark IV, with headlights fared into the fenders.

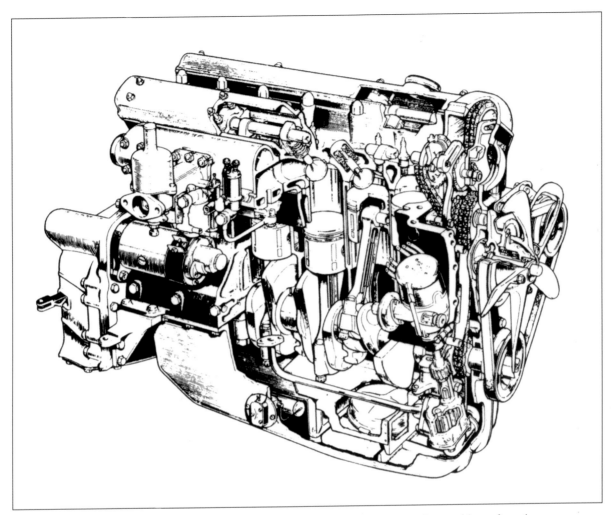

In 1948, Jaguar introduced the 3.4-liter double overhead cam 6-cylinder "XK" engine that would transform the company from building modified cars on another's chassis with Jaguar engines, into a full-scale automobile manufacturer. The XK engine had been designed by Lyons, Chief Engineer William Heynes, engine designers Walter Hassan and Claude Bailey while they were on fire watch duty during World War II on the roof of the factory in Coventry.

haul is perhaps the greatest proof of the advances made in design and production in that era."

The XK engine had a bore and stroke of 83 x 106 mm for a capacity of 3,442 cc. and delivered 120 bhp at 5,000 rpm. In experimental form it ran for 24 hours at 5,000 rpm with occasional bursts to as high as 6,000 rpm. The engine's strength may be attributed to the robust and large-diameter seven-bearing crankshaft and the reliability of the valve gear, with two chain-driven camshafts operating two valves per cylinder.

This engine was installed in a box-section frame with great torsional rigidity. The front suspension incorporated torsion bars, while the rear

1949 JAGUAR XK120
Jaguar stunned the sports car world with the introduction of the XK120 in 1948. The sleek lines and skirted rear fenders were unlike anything the world had seen until then. Intended as an interim model to house the 3.4-liter XK engine, the first 240 were built with aluminum bodies. The original engine planned for this car was a 2-liter 4-cylinder engine. But demand was so high for the XK120, that after the first 240 were built, the body was changed to steel for the remainder. The XK120 would be built until 1954.

1953 JAGUAR MARK VII
Jaguar's line in this 1952 *New Yorker* ad included the XK120 Fixed Head Coupe, Roadster and Convertible. Featured was the Mark VII sedan, which included a Borg-Warner automatic transmission for the first time. When the Mark VII was shown at the 1951 New York Auto Show, more than $20 million in orders were received by the importers, Max Hoffman on the East Coast and Charles H. Hornburg Jr. on the West Coast.

used semi-elliptic leaf springs. On the first cars, a V-shaped windshield was fitted, but a small "aero screen" was available for racing. In the rear was a nice-sized luggage compartment, although a 25-gallon fuel tank could be fitted in place of the original equipment 15-gallon tank for longer runs.

After Jaguar built 240 cars with aluminum bodies and demand for the XK120 was still strong, the company switched to steel bodies. In all, from 1948 to 1953 when the XK120 was replaced by the XK140, more than 18,000 were built, with less than 600 going to the home market, confirming the government's export policy.

A 2.4-liter 4-cylinder version of the XK engine was also planned, with the idea of installing it in a "XK100" sports car, but the car was never built. The engine was developed later.

XK120s proved their worth on race tracks. One of the first recorded victories for the car was in the 1949 *Daily Express* race at Silverstone, when Leslie Johnson won and Peter Walker finished second. Johnson also drove the XK120 to its first significant U.S. success in 1950 when he finished second to George Huntoon's Ford-Duesenberg Special in the SCCA's Palm Beach races. John Fitch, who would go on to success as a Mercedes-Benz team driver, was a class winner at Bridgehampton in an XK120 in 1950, as was Erwin Goldschmidt at Westhampton. In June 1950, Clark and Haines finished 12th in Jaguar's first Le Mans effort.

One significant victory, for both car and driver, occurred in August 1950, when a young Stirling Moss won the Tourist Trophy race in Northern Ireland. Here was a major victory for the car and an equally important win for the driver who was soon to make his mark as one of the greatest racing drivers in history.

Jaguar finally introduced the Mark VII sedan (there was no Mark VI because Bentley had a model by that name) with the 3.4-liter XK engine at the London Motor Show in October 1950. When the car was later put on display at the New York Auto Show, dealers placed more than $20 million in orders.

JAGUAR
Mark VII

$4170
At ports of entry;
sales tax, white-wall tires,
automatic transmission
and license extra.

Now with automatic transmission

Now the distinguished continental lines and superlative performance
of the Jaguar are enhanced by the simple utility of the automatic transmission.

Exclusively designed for Jaguar by Borg-Warner, this automatic transmission adds a final
note of distinction to a car already acclaimed for old-world craftsmanship and sports car performance.

Visit your local dealer and enjoy the thrill of a demonstration in the 1953 Jaguar
with automatic transmission. *Then you'll know that Jaguar is the one fine car for you.*

HOFFMAN MOTOR CAR CO., INC.
Importer East of the Mississippi
487 Park Avenue, New York

CHARLES H. HORNBURG, JR., INC.
Importer West of the Mississippi
9176 Sunset Blvd., Los Angeles

Guaranteed factory parts and complete service at dealers in most major cities

THE FINEST CAR OF ITS CLASS IN THE WORLD

 XK-120 Sports Coupe,
sedan comfort with
racing car performance

 XK-120, world's fastest
production car,
132.6 miles per hour

 XK-120 Convertible,
handsomely appointed—120
miles per hour performance
2-251F

The
1950s

Chapter Three

After the less-than-successful first effort at Le Mans in 1950, Jaguar returned a year later with a new car. Labeled the XK120C (or C-type, the "C" was for Competition), the car was a sleek, lightweight, aerodynamic version of the road car. One writer called the C-type body "purposeful-looking and stark." The aluminum body was designed by Malcolm Sayer, who would go on to design other great Jaguar sports cars. The space frame chassis carried an uprated 220 horsepower version of the 3.4-liter XK engine. To reach this level, the compression ratio was raised to 9.0:1 and high-lift camshafts were fitted. A wide choice of gear and axle ratios was available. There was torsion-bar suspension front and rear. The C-type

1953 JAGUAR XK120M
The XK120M (the "M" was for Modified) had an improved 3.4-liter XK engine that delivered 190 horsepower, as opposed to the 160 horsepower of the original. The extra power came from race-bred high-lift camshafts and 8.0:1 compression ratio pistons.

won at Le Mans in 1951 at the record average of 93.5 miles per hour. The car driven by Peter Walker and Peter Whitehead led a team of three cars to overall victory, and the car driven by Stirling Moss and Jack Fairman was leading when the engine failed.

Later in the year, Moss repeated his Tourist Trophy win in Northern Ireland, this time driving a C-type, with Peter Walker finishing second. The car driven by Tony Rolt and Leslie Johnson finished third.

Jaguar expanded on the business side as well, buying the neighboring Daimler factory on Browns Lane, Coventry. Daimler was a company that had descended from the original Daimler company of Germany. While the German company was renamed Daimler-Benz after the 1926 merger of Daimler and Benz and eventually became Mercedes-Benz, the British company retained the Daimler name and regularly supplied limousines and sedans to the Royal Family. Jaguar's purchase of the

33

1953 JAGUAR C-TYPE
In 1951, Jaguar launched an assault on Le Mans with the XK120C, or C-type. The "C" was for Competition. The C-type was a pure racing car, with a space frame chassis made up of steel tubing and an independent rear suspension. The aerodynamic body, designed by Malcolm Sayer, was built of aluminum. Jaguar won the 1951 Le Mans 24 Hours with a C-type driven by Peter Walker and Peter Whitehead. When the 1952 cars retired due to overheating, the car was redesigned slightly for the 1953 race and was made 120 pounds lighter. This 1953 version represents the cars that finished first, second, fourth and ninth in the 1953 race.

factory and the name added significant prestige to the company.

In 1952, the merger of the British manufacturing companies Austin and Morris into the British Motor Corporation had little immediate impact on Jaguar, although BMC did build and distribute Austin-Healey sports cars, which were priced below the XK120.

Jaguar's 1952 Le Mans effort wasn't as successful as 1951, because a new streamlined body designed by Sayer developed cooling problems. All three works cars retired. Later in the year, Phil

JAGUAR XK120 FIXED HEAD COUPE
Jaguar's XK120 Fixed Head Coupe, introduced in 1951, had a remarkable resemblance to the Bugatti Atlantique coupe. Both had long hoods, sweeping fenders, "bullet" headlights, split windshields, and cramped cockpits. The similarities weren't accidental, because William Lyons was an acknowledged fan of the Bugatti and wanted his car to look like it. This XK120 is owned by Les Jackson.

Hill won one of his first races in a C-type sponsored by Jaguar West Coast distributor Charles Hornburg Jr.

The cooling problems were solved for the 1953 Le Mans race. Disc brakes were also added to the cars, which were 120 pounds lighter thanks to the use of lightweight electrical equipment and aircraft-style fuel tanks. With an even more powerful version of the 3.4-liter engine, (Weber carburetors replacing SUs) and a redesigned rear suspension that incorporated a Panhard rod and a torque arm, C-types finished first, second, fourth and ninth, led by the team of Tony Rolt and Duncan Hamilton.

Jaguar had introduced a Fixed Head Coupe (hard top) version of the XK120 in 1951. A Drop Head Coupe version followed in May 1953. The Drop Head was more closely related to an American convertible, with wind-up windows and more creature comforts than the original Open Roadster. The top could be raised and lowered in a matter of seconds, and its bracing structure was completely concealed by a padded and fully lined mohair top. Inside, the Drophead Coupe had a walnut-veneer dash and door trim as did the Fixed Head Coupe.

The Fixed Head Coupe bore a striking resemblance to the Bugatti Atlantique, with the long

JAGUAR XK120 FIXED HEAD COUPE AND XK8 CONVERTIBLE
Jaguar's first Fixed Head Coupe, the XK120, and its newest sports car, the XK8, sit side-by-side in an Alexandria, Virginia, courtyard, displaying the advances in automotive design in 50 years. The XK120 is a "vertical" design, while the XK8 is more "horizontal," showing more attention to aerodynamics. The XK120 is owned by Les Jackson.

hood, horseshoe-shaped grill and flowing hood and fenders. The resemblance is no coincidence. Lyons was an avowed fan of Bugatti designs. In fact, according to XK120 FHC owner Les Jackson, there are reports that when Lyons was informed that the seating capacity in the FHC was cramped, he said he didn't care as long as the Bugatti-like lines were retained.

Jackson also notes that "the design department apparently ran out of pencils when they got to the back of the car." Where the front two-thirds of the car is a pleasant combination of sweeping lines and compound curves, the rear is bland, and appears to have been copied from an Austin-Healey 100 or the yet-to-be-produced MGA.

Despite the use of disc brakes on the Le Mans winning C-type, the XK 120 and later 140 were still supplied with drum brakes. One other feature that indicated the direction the sedans would follow was the addition of a 3-speed automatic transmission for the Mark VII.

1954 JAGUAR XK140
When Jaguar began offering a Borg-Warner 3-speed automatic transmission in the XK140, it may have offended some sports car "purists," but the company was recognizing what modern producers of sport utility vehicles are realizing; not all vehicles are driven the way they are built to be driven. Many XK140 owners used their cars for sporty driving, rather than racing. They would appreciate the convenience of an automatic transmission, especially if they were driving in the Fixed Head Coupe, with its superior weather protection.

Now... the convenience of Borg-Warner
automatic transmission
available in the **Jaguar** XK-140
convertible and hardtop coupe.

1955 JAGUAR D-TYPE 3.8
Replacing the C-type as the company's racer was, the D-type. This car had monocoque construction, as opposed to the space-frame construction of the C-type, with a magnesium alloy tub. While the D-type finished second to a Ferrari in the 1954 Le Mans race, it was credited with winning the disastrous 1955 event, in which more than 80 people were killed. D-types repeated his success in 1956 and 1957, the latter race being under the colors of Ecurie Ecosse, a private racing team.

While the C-type was successful at Le Mans in its first effort, the D-type had no such luck. In 1954, it finished second to a 4.5-liter Ferrari. Success came in the tragic 1955 race, however, when the D-type won after Mercedes-Benz withdrew. Jaguar repeated its win in 1956 with a factory-back D-type and in 1957 with a private entry D-type.

"passenger" seat with a fin behind the driver's head. The cars used higher wraparound windshields and the exhaust exited out the rear. Six cars were built.

Unfortunately, Jaguar's 1955 win was tainted by the accident with Pierre Levegh's Mercedes-Benz 300SL that caromed off Lance Macklin's Austin-Healey and into the crowd, killing more than 80 people. A Mercedes was leading when the company withdrew from the race, handing it to Jaguar.

The D-type was even lighter and more potent (250 bhp) than the C and had an unorthodox frame built around a central welded fabrication. Forward of this center section was a sub-frame to support the engine and front suspension.

Jaguar announced in October 1956 that it was withdrawing from racing as a factory team, but would continue to support private entries.

At the 1955 London Motor Show in October, Jaguar introduced a compact sedan, the 2.4, with a 112 horsepower 2.4-liter version of the venerable XK 6-cylinder engine. With a price of £895 ($1,500) plus tax, the economical sedan offered speeds of over 100 miles per hour and seating for five people in a luxurious leather-lined interior with a walnut-veneer dash.

The year 1956 was important for Jaguar in other ways as well. In recognition of his vast contributions to the British automobile industry, as well as national pride in winning Le Mans with cars from his company, William Lyons became Sir William Lyons early in the year when he was Knighted by Queen Elizabeth II.

That same year, Jaguar introduced the Mark VIII sedan, which was more luxurious than the Mark VII which preceded it. The Mark VIII used walnut veneer throughout the passenger compartment, including two picnic tables for rear-seat passengers. In addition, the car had three cigar/cigarette lighters for smoking passengers, clocks for front and rear passengers, and a veneered magazine rack for rear seat passengers in cars with a bench front seat. Under the bonnet was the 210 horsepower version of the 3.4-liter XK engine.

the car...the Jaguar XK-140 hardtop coupe . . . about to depart from
the Plaza 'midst a modest cloud of admiring glances. For this version of the fabulous "XK"
(there are three models) is considered by automotive aesthetes to be one of the
all-time gems of motor car design. The XK-140 HARDTOP is particularly favored
by business and professional men who make a *pleasure* of the *necessity* of
driving. Cozy, comfortable, luxuriously appointed . . . and, of course,
pure JAGUAR in performance. With additional rear seating accommodation,
priced at approximately $3,900.

For the traveler, may we suggest that you ask your dealer about the "Visit Europe Delivery Plan."
Jaguar Cars North American Corporation, 32 East 57th Street, N. Y. 22, N. Y.
(Importer east of the Mississippi)
Charles H. Hornburg Jr., Inc., 9176 Sunset Blvd., Los Angeles, Cal.
(Importer west of the Mississippi)

195

the Jaguar Mark VII

The stately four door MARK VII SEDAN represents a pinnacle of automotive craftsmanship. Among its many virtues is the ability to carry six people swiftly over great distances . . . in supreme luxury.

The MARK VII is at home on any road . . . in town or country. Throughout the world it is frequently seen proudly bearing license plates marked *Corps Diplomatique.*

The MARK VII is available with automatic transmission and standard equipment includes such amenities as a sliding sun roof, double fuel tanks to allow tremendous luggage capacity . . . lavish yet tasteful use of hand-rubbed walnut panelling and glove leather upholstery.

It is a car that gives its passengers as much pleasure as the owner behind the wheel.

SPECIFICATIONS

- **Engine:** Six cylinder 3½ litre twin overhead camshaft Jaguar XK engine developing 190 H.P. Twin S.U. horizontal carburetors.
- **Transmission:** Borg Warner automatic transmission. Four speed synchromesh gearbox with optional overdrive available on special order.
- **Suspension:** Independent front suspension; transverse wishbones, torsion bars and telescopic shock absorbers. Rear: Half elliptic springs controlled by telescopic shock absorbers.
- **Brakes:** Vacuum servo-assisted hydraulic. Friction lining area 179 sq. ins.
- **Steering:** Recirculating ball. Adjustable steering wheel.
- **Wheels:** Steel disc wheels with Dunlop 6.70 x 16 in. tubeless tires.
- **Fuel Supply:** Twin S.U. electric pumps. Capacity 20½ gallons in two tanks of 9½ and 11 gallons. Turn-over switch on instrument panel.
- **Electrical:** 12 volt 64 amp/hour battery.
- **Instruments:** 120 mph speedometer, tachometer, ammeter, oil pressure, water temperature and fuel gauges, electric clock.
- **Body:** Four door all steel six seater with sliding roof. Built-in heater, defroster and windshield washers. Upholstered in finest quality leather over foam rubber. Polished walnut panels.
- **Luggage Accommodations:** Capacious 17 cubic foot trunk with spare wheel fitted inside.
- **Dimensions:** Wheelbase 10 ft.; overall length 16 ft. 4½ ins.; width 6 ft. 1 in.; height 5 ft. 3 ins.; dry weight 3696 lbs.

1956 2.4, XK140, MARK VII

Jaguar's 1956 brochure showed the versatility of the company, with offerings of a compact sedan—the 2.4, a thoroughbred sports car—the XK140, and a large sedan—the Mark VII. The XK140 and Mark VII were powered by the 3.4-liter XK 6-cylinder engine, while the new 2.4 used a smaller version of the same engine. The 2.4 offered 30 miles per gallon and 100 miles per hour performance in a compact sedan that could comfortabley carry five passengers. The XK140 was the second-generation postwar Jaguar sports car, combining knowledge gained from the XK120 as well as three wins at the Le Mans 24 Hours race. The Mark VII was a full-size sedan with seating for six in "supreme luxury."

1956 XK140 FIXED HEAD COUPE

Jaguar's XK140 Fixed Head Coupe offered the ultimate for the "Man About Town." Here was a sports car of the highest magnitude, yet it was also a closed coupe that would protect the driver and his passenger from the elements. And a rear seat was available. The price was a reasonable $3,900.

1957 JAGUAR XKSS
When Jaguar withdrew from factory racing in 1956, it still had some spare D-type chassis lying around the factory. The solution was to take the cars, equip them with road gear to make them "street legal," and sell them as production cars. These cars were called the XKSS. Unfortunately, a fire in the Jaguar factory on February 12, 1957, wrote the final chapter on the XKSS shortly after the first one had been written. With only 16 cars completed, the remaining stock of XKSS chassis were destroyed in the fire, as well as several sedans. Jaguar returned to production within a week, but the XKSS was never revived.

With the end of factory-backed racing, there were a few D-type chassis lying around the factory. Lyons had an excellent idea what to do with them. The solution was to add bumpers, a muffler and top to the cars to make them suitable for road use and sell them to the public as the XKSS. With a list price in the United States of $5,600, it was expensive, but desirable. Unfortunately, a fire at the Browns Lane factory on February 12, 1957, destroyed most of the XKSS cars that were being built, leaving a production run of just 16. Limited production of regular cars returned to Browns Lane in just two days. Less than two weeks later, the company introduced the 3.4 sedan, which was a larger-engined version of the 2.4. Full production also returned to Browns Lane shortly, but without the XKSS.

The next version of the sports car was the XK150, which was introduced at the New York Auto Show in March 1958. The engine was the 210 horsepower version of the XK 3.4, but servo-assisted four-wheel disc brakes were now available for stopping. The transmission was a 4-speed manual, but a 3-speed automatic was available. An "S" version of the XK150 became available later, with a three-carburetor version of the 3.4-liter engine tuned to D-type specifications and developing 250 horsepower. This

1957 JAGUAR XK150
The XK150 was the ultimate expression of the XK line. While it was heavier and wider than the XK120 and 140, it had a curved one-piece windshield that improved the styling, and power options that helped the 3.8-liter XK engine develop as much as 265 horsepower to improve performance. The XK150 also had wind-up windows, which forced the elimination of the low-cut doors of the XK140.

With sedans as its bread-and-butter line, Jaguar sports cars have always played second fiddle. The problem for the ad people was how to turn this into an advantage. Make it exclusive! Only 7,500 XK150s would be sold in the United States, making it exclusive. And what a car it was. Four-wheel disc brakes, one-piece windshield, roll-up windows and a sensible convertible top made the XK150 as comfortable as any sedan, with a lot more performance than most sedans could offer.

car was only available with a manual transmission, however. All these had rack and pinion steering and disc brakes.

In October 1959, the new 3.8-liter XK engine became available for the XK150. In standard form, this engine developed 220 horsepower, but in "S" tune it pumped out 265 horses.

Along with the XK150, Jaguar also introduced its latest large "Saloon," the Mark IX in October 1958. Powered by the 3.8-liter XK 6-cylinder, and with standard disc brakes and power steering, the Mark IX was a true luxury sedan.

Jaguar introduced Mark 2 versions of the 2.4 and 3.4 sedans in 1959, along with a 3.8-liter version of the compact sedan, also designated Mark 2, even though there was no "Mark 1" 3.8. As they should have, the Mark 2 versions were improved versions of the original cars. Larger glass area gave the A-pillars a slimmer, more attractive line. A wider rear track, designed to improve handling, also eliminated the

Successor to the XK140 was the XK150 (left), with a slightly more bulbous body, but improved interior room. Introduced in 1957, it was built until 1961, by which time it had become the most prolific range ever built by Jaguar to that time. The cockpit was widened by 4 inches and a curved one-piece windshield was fitted in place of the flat two-piece affairs of the XK120 and 140. Top speed for the original XK150 was in excess of 135 miles per hour. In 1959 and afterward, the XK150 was powered by the 3.8-liter version of the XK engine. In standard form this engine developed 220 horsepower, while in "S" form, power was up to 265 horsepower. This XK150 is pictured next to an XKS.

"pinched in" look of the original cars. Up front, standard fog lights were fitted in place of the air intakes. The bigger 3.8-liter engine made the cars more competitive in touring car races and rallies. Automatic and manual gearboxes were offered.

Mark 2s had enviable racing records in British sedan racing, until Ford brought Galaxies over with big honking V-8 engines that Jaguar simply couldn't compete with. Among the drivers were Roy Salvadori, Graham Hill, Jack Sears, Colin Chapman and American Walt Hansgen. Jack Coombs prepared many Mark 2s for racing, including Hansgen's. He recalled Hansgen for this writer when we did an article on the Mark 2 for *Automobile Quarterly*:

"Walt Hansgen was the most exciting driver I have ever seen. I had him over here and he drove my Mark 2. He would go into Woodcote Corner [at Silverstone] absolutely sideways. I asked him what speed he was going and he said, 'John, it's a bit difficult to tell you. I haven't got time to look at the instruments. I'm a little busy.' But Walt was the best Mark 2 driver. He just chucked it sideways. He was a great character."

Jaguar closed out the 1950s in strong form, with a wide variety of cars to offer in a wide variety of classes, from sports cars to large sedan. The following decade, though, would see a period of turmoil for the company, both in the marketplace and in the corporate offices.

JAGUAR 3.4 SEDAN

Jaguar

Versatile beauty. Responsive as a sports car yet meticulously fitted with all the appurtenances of supreme comfort. Tailored for family driving.

1959 JAGUAR 3.4 SEDAN

The 1959 Jaguar 3.4 Sedan offered everything a Jaguar owner would want in a compact sedan. For less than $4,600, a buyer could obtain performance of an XK150 (or at least the same engine and transmission of an XK150) with the traditional luxury of a Jaguar sedan, all in a compact package. There was no mistaking a Jaguar coming at you down the highway, either. With its oval grille and vertical chrome slats flanked by two huge headlights, there was nothing that looked quite like a Jaguar 3.4.

JAGUAR MARK IX SEDAN

Jaguar's Mark IX Saloon, or sedan, was introduced in October 1958, and would be the last "old style" sedan built by Jaguar. The next generation Mark X would be a longer, lower, more aerodynamic vehicle. The Mark IX, though, was a true large luxury sedan, with leather upholstery, walnut veneer dash and the powerful 3.8-liter XK double overhead cam 6-cylinder engine. The Mark IX also had power steering and front disc brakes for stopping. Skirts over the rear wheels aided aerodynamics slightly. As evidence of the market Jaguar was hoping to compete in with the Mark IX, compare this car with a Rolls-Royce of the era and note the strong similarities. The only major difference is in the grille. *Margaret Harrison*

TOP RIGHT
1961 JAGUAR XK150

The last year of production for the XK150 was 1961, when this car was built. The XK150 was available with the 3.8-liter engine that offered exhilarating performance. A choice of transmissions was also offered, with a four-speed manual (with or without overdrive) as standard and a Borg: Warner three-speed automatic as optional. Special Equipment XK150s were available with wire wheels, dual exhausts, fog lamps and windshield washers.

RIGHT
1960 JAGUAR MARK IX

The Jaguar Mark IX sedan showed little exterior change from the Mark VIII. Under the skin, however, there were several changes, prime of which was the installation of a 3.8-liter double overhead cam 6-cylinder engine rated at 225 horsepower. This was also the first Jaguar sedan to be offered with standard front disc brakes and power steering. The engine offered more power, the disc brakes offered the opportunity to stop the two-ton sedan more easily, and the power steering made it possible to handle it more easily.

The
1960s

Chapter Four

Jaguar had established its American ties early, beginning with Lyons' 1948 trip to the United States to set up sales and service agents. Lyons' relationship with importer Max Hoffman soured when Hoffman rejected Lyons advice and began importing Mercedes-Benz cars in 1953. That same year, Jaguar hired Johannes Eerdmans, to set up an import company in Manhattan.

In May 1960, Jaguar bought the Daimler factory at Radford in Coventry for £3.4 million, which became the main production center for engines and suspension units.

1963 JAGUAR E-TYPE

Few cars have had the impact on the world of automobiles as the Jaguar E-type, introduced in 1961. Its sleek aerodynamic lines were unlike anything seen on the road until that time. Designed by Malcolm Sayer, the E-type (or XKE in the United States) was powered by a 265 horsepower 3.8-liter XK engine at first that gave it a top speed in the neighborhood of 150 miles per hour. The E-type also had 4-wheel disc brakes, with the rear brakes mounted inboard.

Jaguar bought Coventry Climax in 1963, gaining an important engine developer. Some rumors said the only reason Lyons bought Coventry Climax was to regain the services of Walter Hassan, who had left Jaguar to work there. By 1965, Jaguar Cars Inc. had become the Jaguar Group, with 20 different companies under the corporate umbrella, including Daimler, Coventry Climax and Guy trucks.

In order to reduce his involvement with the company, Sir William named 16 "executive directors" in June 1966. One month later, Jaguar merged with the British Motor Corporation to form British Motor Holdings (BMH). The idea of the merger, at least in Jaguar's mind, was that BMC's size and assets would provide Jaguar with a sound financial and engineering base. While Sir William still remained in titular control of the company, corporate interests dictated many moves. Lyons relinquished the role of Managing Director to "Lofty" England early in 1968.

The gentlemen are discussing automotive performance. But, as Jaguar owners, they should know better than compare the speed of the new XK-E with that of the 3.8 Sedan, since speed alone has never been the criterion of excellence in judging Jaguars. How, then, you may ask, does one choose between the XK-E and the 3.8 Sedan? Both offer dramatic acceleration, phenomenal performance and superb handling. Therefore, let your own personal require-ments be the basis for your choice between the two. If there are two of you, then by all means investigate the new XK-E. But, if family needs dictate a roomier vehicle, then avail yourself of the comforts and spaciousness of the 3.8 Sedan. Both are, after all, thoroughbred Jaguars. For more information on both of these fine automobiles, consult your nearest Jaguar Dealer, or write JAGUAR CARS INC., 32 East 57th Street, New York 22, N. Y.

The Jaguar XK-E vs. the 3.8 Sedan

1961 XK-E AND 3.8 SEDAN
Both the XK-E (or E-type) and the 3.8 Sedan were powered by the venerable 3.8-liter XK 6-cylinder engine. By 1961, when this ad appeared, the engine was almost 15 years old. It would continue in operation into the 1980s. While the E-type offered stirring sports car performance, the 3.8 Sedan would take the same engine/transmission combination and put it in a compact five-passenger sedan. Nissan called its 1990s Maxima "the four-door sports car." It is a definition that Jaguar could have used 30 years earlier.

Unification of the British automobile industry continued in 1968 when BMH and Leyland Motor Corporation joined, forming British Leyland Motor Corporation. Sir William was named deputy chairman of BLMC under Lord Stokes. The new corporation joined 95 percent of the British-owned motor industry under one banner.

Johannes Eerdmans had been president of the successful Jaguar Cars North America since 1954. He held this position through the formation of British Leyland and retired in 1969. Graham Whitehead, as president of British Leyland Motors Inc., replaced him as Jaguar's U.S. chief.

On the automotive side, the 1960s were highlighted by the introduction and development of the E-type (or XKE in the United States). Rumors of a new and full-blooded Jaguar sports car grew through 1960. Introduced at the Geneva Salon in March 1961, the E-type was an instant success. Designed by Malcolm Sayer, it had some of the lines of the D-type and prototype E2A racer that followed it. But here was a completely new road car with a look unlike any other. The car was introduced in two forms—Open Roadster (or convertible) and Fixed Head Coupe. It was the latter, with its dramatic fastback styling and faired-in headlights, that the public fell in love with.

Powered by a 265 horsepower version of the XK 3.8-liter engine, the E-type had performance

1961 JAGUAR E-TYPE
Jaguar's E-type (or XK-E) hit the sports car world like an A-bomb. It offered stirring styling in both Coupe and Roadster forms, but it was the Coupe that elicited the most excitement. Fastback styling was still fairly new to most Americans, and when they saw the E-type, they went wild. The back door opened to reveal a healthy storage compartment, while the nose tipped forward to reveal the three-carburetor 3.8-liter XK 6-cylinder engine.

to match its good looks. The engine and gearbox were mounted in a detachable fabricated subframe with box-section frame members carrying the coachwork.

The coupe could go from 0-60 miles per hour in seven seconds and had a top speed of 151 miles per hour. It handled, too. The front suspension was by wishbones and torsion bars. Telescopic

Newest of Jaguars: The classic Mark X luxury sedan

As of today, the fine-car connoisseur has nothing left to wish for. Because here, with the introduction of the new Jaguar Mark X Sedan, is luxury rarely equalled; performance without peer. Under way, new monocoque construction and independent rear suspension afford a ride that is nothing short of phenomenal. Appointments are of the finest, and typically Jaguar. Seats are of the finest glove leather, with those in front fully reclining. Cabinet work is of hand-crafted walnut, mated and matched. Walnut tables, each with a vanity mirror, fold rearward from the front seat-backs. Standard equipment includes power-assisted steering, two independent brake systems (power-assisted), dual fuel pumps and lockable dual fuel tanks, automatic transmission with intermediate gear-hold for passing. Look for the Mark X at your Jaguar dealer's or write JAGUAR CARS INC., 32 East 57th St., N. Y. 22, N. Y. Jaguar Technical Service and Parts Headquarters, 42-50 Twenty-First Street, Long Island City 1, New York

1962 JAGUAR MARK X

The 1962 Mark X offered the consumer pure Jaguar luxury and performance at a reasonable price; reasonable when you compare it to a Rolls-Royce which offered slightly more luxury and less performance at a higher price. The Mark X Sedan offered leather seating ("glove soft"), hand-crafted walnut cabinetry, including walnut tables with vanity mirrors on the backs of the front seats, monocoque construction and a fully independent suspension.

JAGUAR XK-Engineering

The Jaguar engine

To the untutored observer, the excitement that is the new Jaguar XK-E very likely begins and ends with a single glance at the long, lithe lines of this dramatic motor car. But the astute autophile realizes that total appreciation requires, among other things, an appraisal of the mighty heart that beats within the XK-E.

Upon opening the massive hood, dyed-in-the-wool Jaguar lovers will recognize an old friend. Modified, improved and increased slightly in capacity, it is still in essence the same thunderous, twin overhead-cam, six-cylinder power plant that has proved its reliability in winning hard-fought victories the world over and has made Jaguar famed and feared on every major racing circuit.

With a displacement of 230.6 cu. in. and a compression ratio of 9 to 1, the Jaguar XK-Engine develops 265 bhp at 5500 rpm, with torque an impressive 260 lbs. ft. at 4000 rpm. The cooling system features a fan which is thermostatically controlled and operates independently of the engine, thereby eliminating fan drag at road speeds. For those interested in such figures, performance translates to 0-60 in 6.4 seconds, 0-100 in 16.0 seconds and time for the standing quarter-mile of 14.6 seconds. Of more importance to the average driver is the fact that, thanks to superior engineering, the XK-Engine may be driven in top gear at speeds of 10-15 mph without a trace of lugging or roughness.

It is important to note that in addition to the rigid inspection of all components during manufacture, each and every Jaguar XK-Engine is individually bench tested prior to installation—a procedure which ensures a performance and dependability second to none in the automotive field. We cordially invite you to view this, and the many other aspects of Jaguar XK-Engineering soon at your local dealer's and discover for yourself why Jaguars are the most advanced automobiles on the road. JAGUAR CARS INC., 32 East 57th St., New York 22, New York.

JAGUAR XK-Elegance

1962 JAGUAR E-TYPE

The essence of the Jaguar E-type was its three carburetor double overhead cam XK 6-cylinder engine. William Lyons always was concerned with the esthetics of his automobiles, whether from the outside or the inside. Consequently, his engines always dazzled the eye when you opened the hood. The 4.2-liter (230.6 cubic inch) engine developed 265 horsepower at 5,500 rpm, or 1.15 horsepower per cubic inch. And yet the XK-E was still elegant enough to accommodate a young lady in a fur coat.

shock absorbers were at all four corners. It is in the final abandonment of the conventional heavy rigid rear axle that this car broke most with Jaguar tradition. The rear suspension was mounted on a sub-frame and was by two pairs of coil springs with universal-jointed half-shafts located by radius arms and transverse links. Dunlop disc brakes were all around, with the rears mounted inboard.

At the time, the sports car market in the United States was a full one, with MGA, TR4, Austin-Healey 3000 and Alfa Romeo at the lower end and the Daimler SP250 somewhere in the middle. The E-type had a list price of $5,595 for the convertible and $5,895 for the coupe.

In the E-type's race debut, Graham Hill drove an Equipe Endeavour car to victory over Roy Salvadori in John Coombs' similar car at Oulton Park. It was the first of many wins for the sleek car.

The year 1961 was a watershed year on the sedan front as well. Jaguar introduced the Mark X in October at the London Motor Show. Here was a sleek modern sedan to replace the classic Mark IX, with a monocoque body that was longer and lower than its predecessors, but built on the same wheelbase. The Mark X used the 265 horsepower 3.8-liter XK engine and independent rear suspension of the E-type to record some impressive statistics for a big car; 0-60 miles per hour in under 11 seconds and a top speed of 115 miles per hour. A 4.2-liter version of the same engine powered the 1965 car, introduced in 1964. While this engine had the same nominal horsepower, a 10 percent increase in torque made it a better performer. Top speed was up to 122 miles per hour.

The same 4.2-liter engine made its debut in the 1965 E-type. Externally, the only distinction between the original cars and the 4.2 was a small badge on the trunk lid. Inside, there were new seats that were more comfortable and the elimi-

Five minutes behind the wheel will tell you why the 1964 Jaguar XK-E is the new standard by which all sportscars are compared.

For one thing, it doesn't look like any other car you have ever seen. And it is capable of phenomenal speed and acceleration.

Yet its handling qualities give you the relaxed confidence of always being in complete command,

The sportscar.

whatever the road, speed or driving conditions.

What's more, the 32 unique performance and luxury features of the XK-E are on each car when you buy it. With many other sports cars, they are added "extras."

A few of these features: the race-proven engine; "Monocoque" body; all-around independent suspension; four-wheel disc brakes;

bucket seats fully covered with genuine leather; completely instrumented dash panel.

See and drive the Jaguar XK-E. Roadster; $5,525 P.O.E. Coupe $200 more. (If you're going to Europe, inquire about Jaguar's money-saving Overseas Delivery Plan.) There are Jaguar dealers coast-to-coast. Jaguar Cars Inc., New York 22, N. Y.

The 1964 Jaguar XK-E

1964 JAGUAR E-TYPE
The 1964 Jaguar E-type (or XK-E) Coupe was priced at $5,525 in the United States. As such, it was probably one of the best values for the dollar. It offered the most aerodynamic body of its time, with wire wheels, leather seats, 4-wheel disc brakes, fully independent suspension and monocoque construction.

nation of brushed aluminum trim on the dash and transmission tunnel. Even with the automatic transmission installed after 1966, the E-type 4.2 would accelerate from 0-60 miles per hour in under 9 seconds and reach a top speed of over 136 miles per hour.

In October 1963, Jaguar introduced improved versions of the 3.4 and 3.8 Mark 2, calling them the 3.4S and 3.8S. These cars were 6 inches longer overall to accommodate the independent rear suspen-

sion. This extra length was used to good advantage by increasing the luggage capacity and providing for dual fuel tanks. Interior room improved as well, with the real benefit going to rear seat passengers.

Jaguar introduced yet another variation of the E-type, the 2+2 Coupe, in March 1966. Built on a chassis that was lengthened by 9 inches, the new car had rear seats that were usable by children or one adult on a long run. In addition, the roofline was raised 2 inches, which improved rear headroom. The extra 220 pounds of weight raised 0-60 miles per hour acceleration times to 8.3 seconds, though.

In a marriage between the large sedans and the compact versions, Jaguar introduced the 420 and 420G in October 1966. This car retained the general profile of the S-Class cars, but with a rectangular grille reminiscent of the Mark X. "Eyebrows" over the four headlights were another carryover from the S-type, although American versions had four equal-size headlights. In Europe the inner lights were smaller in diameter. The engine in the 420 was a two-carburetor version of the E-type's three-carburetor engine, delivering 245 horsepower.

While the 420 was derived from the S-Types, the 420G was clearly a derivative of the Mark X. The 420G had a wheelbase that was over a foot longer than the 420 (120 inches vs. 107.3 inches) and was 14.3 inches longer overall (202 inches vs. 187.7 inches). Walnut veneer was used on the dash, which was one of the last to feature toggle switches for controls. These "unsafe" switches would soon be replaced by the "safer" rocker switch variety. The chrome horn ring would also disappear shortly.

At the New York Auto Show in the spring of 1968, Jaguar displayed the Piranha, which was a Bertone-bodied E-type 2+2. The chassis was modified slightly to take D-type wide-rim wheels and wider tires. After appearing at the show and another in Montreal, the car was auctioned by Parke-Bernet

1965 JAGUAR E-TYPE

By 1965, when this E-type was built, the engine capacity had been increased to 4.2 liters, although power was still 265 horsepower. Engine capacity was increased by increasing the bore by 5 mm. A new block was thus needed, which also required a new crankshaft. Jaguar used the cylinder head from the 3.8-liter engine, which did not match exactly with that of the 4.2. Inside, the only difference between this car and the original were new, more comfortable seats and the elimination of the polished aluminum trim around the dash and transmission tunnel.

1967 JAGUAR 3.4 SEDAN
While Jaguar had always built large sedans, the 2.4 and 3.4 (and later 3.8) were the company's first "mid-size" sedans. The first sedans were introduced in 1957, with "Mark 2" versions introduced two years later. The Mark 2 cars offered better visibility with more glass and thinner A-pillars. The 3.4-liter inline six engine developed 210 horsepower, giving it one horsepower per cubic inch displacement. The Mark 2 3.4 was then one of the world's first muscle cars. Wire wheels were offered as a factory option.

1966 JAGUAR E-TYPE
By 1966, when this Series III Jaguar E-type was built, federal regulations had eliminated the faring over the headlights and created a "chromier" grille. The car still retained its aerodynamic lines, although a more vertical windshield detracted somewhat from this. In order to overcome this loss of aerodynamics, the Series III cars were equipped with a 5.3-liter V-12 engine, the first production V-12 to appear since the Cadillacs of the 1930s. The engine was rated at 250 horsepower in the United States, and could be mated to a 4-speed manual or 3-speed automatic transmission.

Galleries. It brought $16,000 at a time when Jaguars were selling for $5,500 to $6,500.

While the large 420G remained in production, all the other Jaguar sedans were made obsolete with the introduction of the XJ6 in September 1968. Through the 1960s, Jaguar was building two completely different lines of sedans in addition to a range of three sports cars. This created a terrific strain on the company's resources. The solution was the XJ6, a mid-size sedan that replaced both existing sedan lines. It was a hit from the start. Here was a car that looked like the 420, but was sleeker and moved Jaguar in a new direction. With the traditional "Jaguar look," it was both trim and modern. While not as big as the Mark X, it was comfortable enough for five adults and offered infinitely better handling

and overall performance. Before the XJ6, Jaguar was a producer of sports cars and high performance sedans; after the XJ6 it was a producer of luxury cars.

Powered by the 4.2-liter XK engine that delivered 245 horsepower, the XJ6 made its mark by having low levels of noise, vibration and harshness years before "NVH" became a watchword for car engineers. Adding to the package were low-profile radial tires,

which, with the independent front and rear suspensions mounted on sub-frames, added to the car's road silence. The dash featured burl walnut trim, eight round instruments and an imposing array of ten toggle switches splayed across the bottom of the dash.

Economy versions of the S-Type—the 240 and 340—were introduced in October 1967. While they retained the basic styling of the Mark 2 sedans,

1967 JAGUAR 340
In 1967, Jaguar introduced "economy" versions of the Mark II sedans, dubbed 240 and 340. This 340 was powered by the venerable 3.4-liter dohc XK six. While the exterior "bathtub" lines of the 340 were almost identical to those of its predecessors, economy was introduced with Ambla vinyl, rather than leather, upholstery. The bumpers were single chrome bars rather than the double bars of the Mark II sedans, and wire wheels were no longer available. The owner of this 340 is Jim Spooner.

the 240 and 340 were truly low-price versions of a medium-priced car. For example, while the 2.4 and 3.4 had leather upholstery, the newer cars were trimmed in Ambla vinyl. The bumpers were slimmer single chrome bars, as opposed to the double bars of the Mark 2. And wire wheels were not available; steel discs were the order of the day. The 240 did get a power boost, though, from 122 horsepower of the original version to 133 in the 240.

Late in 1968, Jaguar introduced the Series II E-type, with modifications made necessary by U.S. Federal Safety regulations. The glass fairings on the headlights were removed in 1967 and the toggle switches replaced by rockers. For the Series II, the headlights were moved forward and the bumpers made more sturdy. A connection with history disappeared when the ears had to be removed from the wire wheel knock-offs, again as a safety measure. Clean air regulations dictated a replacement of the S.U. carburetors with Zenith-Strombergs, which

were cleaner. Thus restricted, the engine now delivered 246 horsepower vs. 265 in the "SU" version.

In the United States, Jaguar headquarters were located on the 12th floor of 32 East 57th Street, New York, where they had been since the late 1950s. Graham Whitehead was named president of Jaguar's U.S. operations in October 1968. Jaguar moved its headquarters to the British Leyland offices to Leonia, New Jersey. Jaguar would retain the location after the dissolution of British Leyland in the 1970s.

Briggs Cunningham had persuaded Jaguar to sell him the E2A prototype car, which was an evolutionary step between the D-type and E-type. Cunningham raced the car at Le Mans with no success, then brought it back to the United States. Painted in Cunningham's white-with-blue-stripes racing colors, it won at Bridgehampton with Walt Hansgen at the wheel. Cunningham then retired the car to his collection in California and sold it to the Collier Museum in Naples, Florida, in 1988.

Jaguar compact sedans, from the 3.4 through the 3.4 Mark II to the final iteration of the 340, were powered by the 3.4-liter dohc XK six. By the time the engine was installed in the 1967 340, it was more than 20 years old, but it had only reached middle age. The engine would continue to power Jaguars into the 1980s, although enlarged ultimately to 4.2 liters capacity. Crammed in the 340, though, it was a service nightmare even in an era of minimal additions for air conditioning and emissions controls.

The 340 was conceived and delivered as an "economy" version of the 3.4 Mark II compact sedan. These economies reached inside the car in the form of vinyl upholstery rather than the original leather and thinner padding in the seats. The burl walnut veneer dash, however, was retained from the Mark II sedans, as were the traditional round, white-on-black instruments. From the left, the instruments are speedometer, tachometer, water temperature, oil pressure, fuel level and battery amperage. Beneath the dash was a small tray that was useful for carrying maps.

With a rear end similar to the Mark I sedans, the only difference exhibited with the 340 was a thinner chrome bumper and chrome farings around the taillights. Even with the smooth rear end that has none of the aerodynamics of modern sports sedans, the Mark IIs and 340s were potent racing cars at the hand of such luminaries as Graham Hill and Roy Salvadori.

Chapter Five | The 1970s

The decade of the 1970s would see Jaguar, and all manufacturers, forced to deal with ever more stringent U.S. Federal safety and emissions legislation. These regulations would cripple engine performance until designers learned how to cope by offering more efficient fuel injection systems. In addition, styling would suffer to some degree with the addition of stronger bumpers and minimum headlight heights.

Jaguar had responded to these rules in the 1960s by modifying the E-type's headlights, for example, in the Series II cars. As that decade ended the glass headlight fairings had disappeared and more substantial bumpers changed the front fascia.

To improve the power situation, Jaguar introduced the Series III E-type in March 1971 with the first V-12 engine in series production since the Lincolns of the 1940s. The 5.3-liter V-12 in the E-type delivered 272 horsepower in Europe and 250 in the U.S. The introduction of the V-12 also meant universal use of the 9 inch-longer "2+2" wheelbase on all models.

The V-12 engine was based on a 5.0-liter concept used in the XJ13 racing prototype. The production version was an all-aluminum 5.3-liter engine with single overhead cams on each bank of cylinders. It was capable of propelling the E-type to 100 miles per hour in 15.5 seconds. Automotive writers all over the world have called the Jaguar V-12 "one of the world's great engines." In fact, its existence was denied for years by Jaguar until it was eventually restored after a

1978 JAGUAR XJ6
While Jaguar has been revered and respected as a producer of high-performance sports cars, it is the Jaguar sedans that have been the bread-and-butter cars. Jaguar introduced the XJ6 in 1968, which was a successful marriage between the compact Mark 2 range and the larger 420 sedans. Powered by a 4.2-liter XK 6-cylinder engine, the XJ6 packaged traditional Jaguar values in a sedan that was years ahead of its time. Five people could ride in comfort in the XJ6, which used the same subframe-mounted rear suspension of the E-type, as well as the E-type's inboard rear disc brakes.

1973 JAGUAR V-12
The Series II E-types lost some of their aerodynamic penetration to a more vertical windshield and uncovered headlights. But still they were unmatched by any other cars on the road at the time. With the 5.3-liter V-12 engine under the hood, the E-type could accelerate from 0-60 miles per hour in 6.8 seconds and reach a top speed that was illegal in any state in the union. But with the smoothness of the V-12, you could also cruise at 10 miles per hour in top gear and accelerate to cruising speed.

1976 JAGUAR XJC COUPE
When Jaguar introduced the Series II XJ sedans, the company also introduced coupe versions in both six and V-12-engined versions. The cars were introduced in 1973, but weren't available until 1974. The reason for the delay was that the pillarless door design did not seal perfectly at high speed. By 1976, the Coupes also had to compete with the new XJS. Add to this the fact that the Coupes cost $750 more than the Sedans, and sales weren't what was expected.

the rear brakes mounted inboard, as in the E-Type, to reduce unsprung weight. Long wheelbase versions of both the XJ6 and XJ12 were introduced just two months later. These cars offered an extra 4 inches in wheelbase and 2 inches in overall length to improve rear seat leg room. With a 4-inch longer rear door, entry and exit also became easier.

Series II versions of Jaguar's entire XJ sedan line were introduced in September 1973. These redesigns were required to satisfy U.S. safety regulations which dictated a front bumper height of 16 inches. Since this would have put the bumpers in the middle of the XJ grille, the front end was redesigned. And as some reporters of the scene noted, the change lightened the look of the Jaguar

PRESENTING THE SUPERB NEW JAGUAR XJ-S

1976 XJS
Jaguar introduced the XJS in 1976, saying it had "the performance and handling of the more expensive sports cars and the quietness and comfort of luxury sedans." Maybe it was the quietness and comfort that made purists dislike the XJS. However, it was powered by the same 5.3-liter V-12 that had powered the E-type. Standard equipment included an 8-track AM/FM stereo sound system and a heated rear window.

front end, while similar changes to cars including the MGB and Triumph Spitfire served to destroy the looks of the cars.

The dash of the Series II XJ was also redesigned to replace the confusing, if handsome, array of rocker switches in front of the driver with a more logical arrangement. Instruments were now clustered in front of the driver in a redesigned instrument panel.

Two-door versions of the XJ sedans—XJ6C and XJ12C—were introduced along with the

Series II sedans. Due to a combination of problems, these cars did not sell well and were discontinued in 1975. With their windows down, these 2-door "hardtop" coupes looked like convertibles with their tops raised. This look was enhanced by the standard vinyl top of the coupes.

One of the reasons for dropping the XJ coupes was the introduction of the XJ-S sports coupe in September 1975. Initially shown at the Frankfurt Auto Show with a V-12 engine, the XJ-S was the last product to show the design hands of Sir

69

1977 JAGUAR XJS
By 1975, the E-type had been around for almost 15 years and was getting stale. Jaguar needed a new sports car to replace it, but the era of sports cars was also getting stale. The car that replaced the E-type was the XJS, which was introduced in September 1975. Powered by a 5.3-liter V-12 engine, the XJS was a 2+2 coupe with controversial "flying buttresses" around the rear window. While its styling was not universally admired, the XJS would survive for over 20 years and become the most-produced Jaguar sports car of all time.

William Lyons and Malcolm Sayer, who had died in 1970. This sports coupe filled the hole vacated by the E-type, which was discontinued in February 1975. But it was not a sports car in the sense the E-type coupes were. Rather, the XJ-S was more of a grand touring coupe in execution and use, although performance versions of the car did have some racing successes in the United States and Europe.

In true sports car tradition, though, the original XJ-S had a plain interior with leather upholstery. The car would remain essentially unchanged until 1982,

SIR WILLIAM LYONS (LEFT) AND SIR JOHN EGAN (RIGHT)
John Egan took over the reins of Jaguar in 1980, when Sir Michael Edwardes was appointed chairman of British Leyland. Sir William Lyons had an opportunity to meet Egan shortly after the latter took over. Egan was knighted in 1986 for his efforts in resuscitating Jaguar and saving it from the liquidators.

1978 XJ12
The most elegant Jaguar sedan was the XJ12, with the 5.3-liter V-12 engine, 3-speed GM automatic transmission, 4-wheel disc brakes, independent suspension all around, and such traditional Jaguar touches as walnut interior trim, leather seats and power-assisted rack-and-pinion steering. Dual fuel tanks made every trip to the gas station a thrill for the attendant, as did oil changes with the gleaming chrome head covers on the V-12 engine.

tion operating, which meant that the NEB had a major voice in day-to-day operations. Geoffrey Robinson resigned as managing director of Jaguar. Lord Ryder left the NEB in 1977, but the damage had been done. Michael Edwardes was named to head British Leyland (BL) in 1977 with a brief to restore it to profitability by virtually any means. A BL operations committee ran Jaguar until Bob Knight was named managing director in 1979. John Egan was hired as managing director by Michael Edwardes in 1980 and Knight retired at that time.

The Ryder Report's misguided attempt to centralize design, engineering and management functions by British Leyland nearly destroyed the spirit that existed in the individual car companies. At Jaguar, a core of people, primarily in engineering, kept the spirit of the company alive as well as the future model program.

when a High Efficiency version appeared. There were complaints about the styling of the XJ-S. which featured "buttresses" around the rear windows that limited rearward vision somewhat.

Powered by a 5.3-liter V-12 engine rated at 244 horsepower, the XJ-S had a top speed of over 135 miles per hour and looked as if it was going that speed even when standing still. One of the reasons for this was a unique styling feature of "flying buttresses" that swept from the roofline to the tail of the car. While these controversial buttresses aided the stability of the XJ-S at speed, they did reduce rearward vision.

Earlier in 1975, a British government report by the National Enterprise Board (NEB), named after its author, Lord Ryder, proposed uniting all British Leyland car manufacturing under one umbrella group, BL Cars. Government funding had to be provided to keep the crippled corpora-

GROUP 44 V-12 E-TYPE AT ROAD ATLANTA
Jaguar's return to racing in the United States was under the banner of Bob Tullius' Group 44 on the East Coast and Joe Huffaker on the West Coast. The Tullius effort was the more successful. Tullius first raced a V-12-engined E-type and was successful in his second year out, winning an SCCA National Championship.

Tullius went to a highly modified XJS after the E-type and won the SCCA's Trans-American Sedan Championship. All Group 44 cars were noted for their pristine finish. With Quaker State as a prime sponsor besides British Leyland, the cars were painted white with two shades of green as a bottom color.

Bob Knight, among others, fought to keep Jaguar engineering dedicated to Jaguar, rather than part of a corporate homogenization. While this ran counter to the aims of the Ryder Report, it was successful and Jaguar engineering remained independent. One of their tactics was to design the engine bay of the forthcoming XJ40 sedan so that it was too narrow to accommodate a Rover V-8, as BL wanted, and they would have to use a Jaguar straight six. Of course, when Jaguar eventually decided to add a V-12 to the line, this plan backfired.

On the competition front, Jaguar Cars Inc. in the United States supported two racing efforts, one under the tutelage of Bob Tullius' Group 44 on the East Coast and the other under Joe Huffaker on the West Coast. Tullius and Lee Mueller in the Huffaker car both drove E-types, with Tul-

1979 XJ6/12, XKS (S-TYPE)

By 1979, Jaguar was calling the XKS the "S-type" in an attempt to place it in the lineage of the C-type, D-type and E-type. The XKS wasn't a sports car in the classic sense; it had far more refinement and probably as good performance as most sports cars. The XKS used the 5.3-liter V-12 engine, which was enough to give it a certain panache. That engine was also available in the Jaguar Sedan, be it XJ6 or XJ12. In these two cars, Jaguar offered stirring performance and unmatched luxury.

lius' overall effort being the more successful. He finished second in the SCCA runoffs at Road Atlanta that year.

Tullius won the SCCA championship in 1975, competing against the likes of Corvette. He switched to an XJ-S in 1976 and won the SCCA's Trans-Am Sedan Championship in 1977 and

1979 JAGUAR XJ-S

"The most extravagant Jaguar ever built" was the elegant 1979 XJ-S. This was the street version of the car that, in Bob Tullius' hands, won five Trans-Am races in its first season. Yet here was also a four-passenger car with fully independent suspension, 4-wheel disc brakes, power rack-and-pinion steering and Jaguar's 5.3-liter V-12 engine.

1978. In the latter year he won seven of ten races. Tullius' final Trans-Am effort was in 1981 when he finished second, but by then the company's efforts were trending toward sports racing cars.

Another competition effort gave Jaguar a record that is likely to stand forever. It was in the 1979 Cannonball Baker Sea-to-Shining-Sea Memorial Trophy Dash from Darien, Connecti-cut, to Los Angeles. Begun by *Car and Driver* Editor Brock Yates early in the decade, it was both a tribute to the erstwhile Cannonball Baker, who set coast-to-coast records in the early years of the century in a variety of cars from Stutz to Cadillac, and it was also a challenge to the national 55 miles per hour speed limit. Yates and a group of competitors would try to be the first to reach Los Angeles.

In the fifth running of the event in 1979, Jaguar dealers Dave Yarborough and Dave Heinz ran the Cannonball in an XJ-S V12 coupe. They covered the 3,000-mile distance in 32 hours, 51 minutes, for an average speed of 86.7 miles per hour. Since it was also the last running of the Cannonball, Heinz' and Yarborough's record will stand forever.

Jaguar closed out the decade of the 1970s with the introduction of Series III versions of the XJ sedan range. With a new roofline and rear window to improve rear seat headroom, the Series III cars showed subtle styling changes which served to perfect the XJ design. Besides the roofline, the side windows slanted in slightly to a narrower roof, the windshield was slanted more sharply, and the wing windows were eliminated. Up front, the horizontal chrome bars of the grille were replaced by vertical bars, which continue to the 1997 models.

In Europe, the new XJ-S became available in 1984 with a choice of engines: a new 3.6-liter six, or the 5.3-liter V-12. In the U.S., however, only the V-12 was offered. Initially rated at 289 horsepower, power output grew to 295 horsepower in 1981. When fuel consumption concerns threatened to kill the V-12, the "Fireball" cylinder head of Swiss engineer Michael May was incorporated into the 1982 "HE" or High Efficiency versions of the engine.

Chapter Six | The 1980s

The 1980s began with Jaguar doing business as usual; moving through a period of rediscovered independence; and ending dramatically with the company under control of Ford and producing the fastest production car of the time. Jaguar returned to the scene of its greatest triumphs at Le Mans and took the prize home twice. On the sad side, founder Sir William Lyons died in February 1985.

Administratively, Jaguar Cars Ltd. ended its unhappy alliance with British Leyland by going public on June 29, 1984. Hamish Orr-Ewing was named chairman of the company, only to be ousted in 1985. John Egan continued through the decade as managing director, retiring in 1990.

1980 JAGUAR XJS
While Jaguar sales were suffering under the confused management of British Leyland in the early 1980s, the XJS continued to carry the banner of Jaguar sports cars. Bob Tullius campaigned an XJS to win the 1978 SCCA Trans-Am Sedan Championship in the V-12-engined car. A 6-cylinder version of the XJS was to come in 1985, but this 1980 car still used the elegant 5.3-liter V-12.

Jaguar production increased from 14,000 at the beginning of the decade to more than 50,000 in 1988, before the U.S. stock market crash of October 1987 put a crimp in all luxury car sales. American sales reached a peak of 24,464 in 1986

In 1984, 178 million Jaguar shares were offered on the British stock market for the first time, with the exception of a "Golden Share" held by the British government to protect the company from a takeover. The offering caused a rush on the London Exchange on August 3, 1984, when there were offers for eight times as many shares as were available. The price of the shares went to £1.88 ($2.94) within a week. In the United States, the over-the-counter price rose to $9.50 in early 1987.

A takeover at the time seemed unlikely. Profits rose to £120.8 million ($189 million) in 1986 and continued near the £100 million ($150 million) mark for several years. A new Engineering Centre was opened at Whitley, Coventry, in 1988. Jaguar Cars Inc., moved to new headquarters in the United States in June

1989 JAGUAR VANDEN PLAS MAJESTIC
Along with the introduction of the new AJ6 engine, Jaguar also introduced the Majestic version of the XJ6 Vanden Plas sedan in 1989. The Majestic only came in Regency Red and included a magnolia leather interior, alarm system and diamond-polished alloy wheels. It also included all the standard Vanden Plas features, such as a limited-slip differential, self-leveling suspension, and folding burl walnut picnic tables on the backs of the front seats.

1990. The new home office was located in Mahwah, New Jersey, in the north-central area of the state, near the New York border.

But all was not completely well. Profits dipped to £47.5 million ($74 million) in 1988, and £1.4 million in the first six months of 1989. In 1989, new competitors appeared from the Far East in the form of luxury cars introduced by the three major Japanese auto manufacturers: Honda's Acura, Toyota's Lexus and Nissan's Infiniti divisions.

John Egan realized that he no longer had the resources to fund product development on his own. Late in 1988, Egan met with Donald Petersen of Ford. Discussions broke off when it was apparent that Ford wanted a majority interest in Jaguar. Egan next went to General Motors. These discussions were more fruitful and GM agreed to an arrangement whereby it would buy 30 percent of Jaguar, but would leave the company independent.

After the brief courtship between Jaguar and GM during 1988, Ford came back into the picture and announced on September 19, 1989, that it would buy 15 percent of Jaguar's stock. Under American regulations and Jaguar articles of incorporation, this was the limit. Such a move also had to be made public. Three weeks later, GM made the same announcement. All this speculation fueled interest in Jaguar shares on the stock market, raising the price from around $5 to around $13.

FASTMASTERS JAGUAR XJ220
While the XJ220 didn't make it to production, approximately a dozen of these cars were used for a one-year racing series called FastMasters. Retired drivers such as Bobby Allison, Parnelli Jones and Jack Brabham raced in events that were companion races to NASCAR or CART events. The series proved to be popular and had TV sponsorship, but the costs of maintaining the cars far exceeded the public relations value.

On October 31, 1989, the British government withdrew its "Golden Share," permitting full takeover of Jaguar. GM had only wanted a minority interest in Jaguar; Ford had decided it wanted the whole package. Ford's offer was now the only acceptable one. On November 2, 1989, Ford purchased Jaguar for £8.50 ($13.28) per share or $2.5 billion (£1.6 billion). The transaction became official on January 1, 1990, when Jaguar Cars Ltd. became a wholly owned subsidiary of the Ford Motor Company.

John Egan told employees of Jaguar North America, "In 1980 when I became chairman of Jaguar, the company was worth nothing. It was a case of revive Jaguar or close it. In 1984, after four years of sales growth worldwide, when we floated our shares, the new worth was approximately $500 million. That in itself was not a bad turnaround. Now in 1989, the Jaguar board has approved an offer from Ford Motor Company of approximately

two and one half billion dollars for Jaguar. That represents a five-fold increase in value since 1984."

Jaguar supported two competition efforts through the early years of the decade, but ended the decade backing just one team worldwide. Bob Tullius and Group 44 continued to be the corporate standard-bearer in the United States. After winning SCCA National Championships in the V-12-powered E-type and two Trans-Am Sedan Championships in the XJS, in 1982 Tullius received permission from Mike Dale of Jaguar Cars to build a prototype racer to compete in the International Motor Sports Association's GTP series in the United States. The car was the XJR-5 (XJ for experimental Jaguar, R for racer, 5 because it was the fifth Jaguar racer for Tullius). The body was designed by Len Dykstra, while the V-12 engine was derived from the 5.4-liter unit used in the XJ-S. In developed 525 horsepower. It its first race, the XJR-5 finished third at Road America. Its first win came in 1983 at Road Atlantic.

1988 LE MANS 24-HOUR VICTORY
Jaguar returned to the Le Mans winner's circle in 1988 with a three-car team of Tom Walkinshaw Racing cars sponsored by Silk Cut and Castrol. The winning car was driven by Johnny Dumfries, Jan Lammers and Andy Wallace, and the three remaining Jaguar cars in the race crossed the finish line after 24 hours in formation.

In Europe, Jaguar support went to Tom Walkinshaw Racing. Walkinshaw raced an XJ-S in the European Touring Car championship and won the title in 1984. Although Tullius spearheaded Jaguar's return to Le Mans in 1985 with a 13th place finish, it was TWR which would be competing in the World Sportscar Championship, which included Le Mans. An XJR-5 was shipped to TWR for analysis, but Walkinshaw had already commissioned a new design from Tony Southgate. Christened XJR-6, the car finished third in its first race at Mosport. Its first win was at Silverstone in May 1986. Group 44 and TWR would continue to build XJR racers, with Group 44 getting the odd numbers and TWR the even numbers.

Group 44 debuted its new car, XJR-7, at Daytona in 1985, where it finished fourth. Tullius and Chip Robinson won the December Daytona three-hour race that year, however. They won two more races in 1987, after it was announced that TWR would also campaign for Jaguar in the United States in 1988. The final race for Group 44 was at Watkins Glen, where there was an emotional "good-bye party" after the race.

For TWR, the 1987 car was the XJR-8, with a 7-liter V-12. The car won eight of ten world championship races and the World Championship of Sports Cars. In 1988 TWR won the Daytona 24 hours and brought Jaguar back to the winners' podium at Le Mans, after 31 years. The driving team of Johnny Dumfries, Jan Lammers and Andy Wallace was successful for Jaguar and TWR.

In February 1990, a TWR XJR-12 won the 24 Hours of Daytona in its first race, driven by Lammers, Andy Wallace and Davy Jones. Jaguar repeated its Le Mans win in 1990 in a car driven by John Nielson, Price Cobb and Martin Brundle. Lammers, Wallace and Franz Konrad finished second in another XJR-12.

In production cars, Jaguar developed a new 3.6-liter 6-cylinder engine that debuted in September 1983. Dubbed the AJ6 (for Advanced Jaguar), this engine would be used initially in the sport coupes, but would later also be used in sedans.

With a capacity of 3,592cc and dual overhead camshafts, the AJ6 was only slightly larger than the XK engine developed during World War II that had been so instrumental in Jaguar's resurgence. Compression ratio for the AJ6 was 9.6:1 and it developed 221 horsepower at 5,000 rpm initially with four valves per cylinder. Eventually, 2.9-liter, 3.2-liter and 4.0-liter versions of this engine would be developed, with the different capacities dictated by changing the stroke from 74.8 to 102 mm, but keeping the bore at 91 mm.

The first cars to use the AJ6 were the 1984 XJ-S line of cars (coupe and cabriolet). The cabriolet

The 1990s

Jaguar showed in the 1990s that it was a company that could rebound and still innovate. Customer Satisfaction Index (CSI) ratings rose from a low of 25th overall in 1992 to 9th overall in 1996, an increase attributable to better production methods and a better corporate attitude toward its customers.

Jaguar was also honored when an E-type roadster was made part of the permanent display at the Museum of Modern Art in New York in 1996, recognizing the car's contribution to the world of automobile styling. Only the third automobile to enter the museum's collection, the Malcolm Sayer-designed car was the showpiece

1996 XJR
Originally introduced in 1995, the XJR carried a Roots supercharged version of the 4.0-liter V-6 that delivered 322 horsepower and 378 pounds-feet torque. The XJR was developed as a joint venture between Jaguar and Tom Walkinshaw's JaguarSport. It represented Jaguar's first supercharged car. Besides superior performance, the XJR also offered increased levels of luxury over the XJ6, with maple wood trim and a wood-and-leather steering wheel.

of a four-month exhibit, "Refining the Sports Car: Jaguar's E-type." Terence Riley, chief curator, Department of Architecture and Design, said," Since 1972, when the Museum acquired its first car, a Cisitalia 202 GT, we have been committed to expanding this facet of the design collection. We developed a wish list of ten to twelve cars, with the E-type at the top. Because of the E-type's beauty and sculptural quality, its functionality, and its seminal impact on overall car design, it perfectly suits the criteria of a landmark design object."

In March 1990, Sir John Egan announced that he would be leaving Jaguar in June of that year after ten years as managing director. His contributions to the company were recognized with his Knighthood, conferred in 1986. Egan also presided over the difficult transition from independent company to Ford subsidiary. After his retirement, Bill Hayden was appointed chairman and chief executive at Jaguar by Ford.

1990 JAGUAR XJ6
For the 1990 XJ6 sedan, Jaguar introduced a 4.0-liter version of the AJ6 engine that was based on the original 3.6-liter AJ6. The XJ6 showed only minor changes from the 1989 edition, as the changes were made in the engine compartment. The influence of Ford management had yet to be felt in the design and development of Jaguar cars. Teves anti-lock brakes replaced the Girling/Bosch units formerly used. Quad round headlights were retained on the base model, but rectangular headlights were used for the Vanden Plas, Sovereign and Majestic.

Hayden, a career production man, announced that the pursuit of quality would be unrelenting, and he set out to achieve this on all fronts. The work force was streamlined and contracts re-negotiated to achieve greater worker commitment to building better products. Investments were made in manufacturing facilities, creating improvements in everything from welding to final painting. An increased number of computer-controlled processes ensured accuracy. More robots on the line also contributed to increased accuracy. Qual-

ity standards were set for suppliers as well, and new suppliers were found for parts that didn't measure up. Ford's buying power helped reduce costs.

White coated inspectors, who stood at the end of the line to evaluate cars, were replaced by fault diagnosis on the line itself. Problems were solved at the source so that finished cars could be driven away directly to the transporters. The Uniform Product Assessment System (UPAS) was instituted to ensure that finished Jaguars met the standards of the luxury car buyer, not just production guidelines.

1991 VANDEN PLAS
Only minor changes were reflected in the 1991 XJ6 and Vanden Plas. Both offered leather seats and burl walnut trim, but the Vanden Plas added boxwood inlays in the woodwork and the traditional picnic tables on the rear of the front seats. For 1991, the Vanden Plas was identified by a fluted grille surround and trunk plinth, which were reminiscent of British Daimlers.

In the United States, Jaguar Cars Inc. president Graham Whitehead also retired in 1990 after almost 22 years at the helm. Whitehead had also presided over drastic changes at Jaguar, since he joined the company right after the merger with British Leyland. He was replaced by Mike Dale, who had an equally long tenure and who was responsible for Jaguar's U.S. racing efforts under Bob Tullius. Dale himself was an SCCA champion, driving an Austin-Healey Sprite to that title in 1973.

Dale would direct the company from new North American headquarters in Mahwah, New Jersey. The new facility among the lush foliage of northern New Jersey was a distinct contrast to the Leonia headquarters, which had been inherited from British Leyland Motor Holdings.

On the competition side, Jaguar won Le Mans in 1990, with a TWR XJR-12 driven by John Nielson, Price Cobb and Martin Brundle. It was Jaguar's second win in three years and seventh win overall. The competition season had begun on a strong note as well, with the TWR car winning the Daytona 24 Hours.

In the first half of the decade, Jaguar products were very much the result of Jaguar management; it was only in the latter half of the decade that the influence of Ford began to be felt. Therefore, the company followed a conservative tack with its early vehicles. The first vehicle to be announced was the 4.0-liter version of the XJ6 sedan in September 1990. The engine was based on the 3.6-liter AJ6 engine. Two new models in the sedan range were the Sover-

1991 XJ-S CLASSIC EDITION
Jaguar's 1991 Classic Edition XJ-S Coupe and Convertible both used a 5.3-liter V-12 engine for power, coupled with a 3-speed automatic transmission. The engine was rated at 263 horsepower at 5,350rpm. The XJ-S rode on a 102.0-inch wheelbase and was 191.7 inches long. It weighed 4,050 pounds, but the big V-12 could move it along at a brisk pace. In 1992, Jaguar warranties would increase from three years/36,000 miles to four years/50,000 miles, showing significant confidence in the improved quality of the line.

eign and Vanden Plas Majestic, giving Jaguar four sedan models, all based on the XJ6. The Vanden Plas was an upgrade from the XJ6, with limited-slip differential, self-leveling suspension, headlight washers with heated nozzles, footwell rugs, heated front seats, folding burl walnut picnic tables on the front seat backs, leather-covered seat backs, rear arm rest storage, fog lights and rear reading lamps. The Sovereign added a power sunroof, burl walnut inlays and rear head restraints. The Majestic, which only came in Regency Red, added a magnolia leather interior, diamond-polished alloy wheels and an alarm system.

Base engine for the 1991 XJ-S Coupe and Convertible was the 5.3-liter V-12. A production version of the XJ220 was announced early in 1991, with a turbocharged 3.5-liter V-6. It was priced at £290,000. Jaguar took £50,000 non-refundable deposits on the car and had a full order book. But when the bottom fell out of the collector car market and investors realized that the value of the XJ220 would not appreciate as much as they

had hoped, they tried to reclaim their deposits. Lengthy lawsuits resulted, with Jaguar eventually ending up retaining the deposits.

The last Series III XJ12 sedan left the line at the end of 1992 and went straight to Jaguar's museum. This sedan/engine combination had helped maintain Jaguar's sense of individuality for 20 years, through periods of turmoil. While the V-12 engine may not have been the most practical in an era of fuel crisis and government-mandated fuel economies, it gave Jaguar a definite "halo effect" car whose value far outweighed its negatives.

In 1993, a new sedan range was offered, with approximately one-third new body panels. The changes were made to alter the rigidity for air bag installation. This year, Jaguar identified the Vanden Plas sedan with fluting around the grille and trunk plinth previously used on the short-lived Majestic. This fluting resembled that used on Daimlers. Late in the year, the XJ12 returned with a 6.0-liter V-12 engine.

By 1994, models in the United States were the XJS convertible and coupe with 4.0-liter 6-cylinder and 6.0-liter V-12 engines, the XJ6 and Vanden Plas sedans with 4.0-liter 6-cylinder engines, and the XJ12 sedan with the 6.0-liter V-12. Passenger-side air bags were installed on all models. Prices ranged from $51,750 for the XJ6 to $79,950 for the XJS 6.0L convertible.

By 1995, the first fruits of the Ford investment were realized with a restyled sedan line, a more powerful 6-cylinder engine, and the introduction of Jaguar's first supercharged car, the XJR sports sedan based on the XJ6. The XJR was powered by the 4.0-liter inline six of the XJ6, but with a Roots-type supercharger and a lowered compression ratio. Still, the XJR posted impressive numbers; 322 horsepower at 5,000 rpm and 378 pounds feet torque at 3,050 rpm. XJR carried a price tag

Jaguar's 1994 line was one of the most comprehensive in the company's history. All cars added passenger-side airbags to the driver's side airbags that had been installed since 1993. The sedans were refined with cellular phone pre-wiring, a remote trunk release, and Pirelli P4000E tires on diamond-turned 7x16 aluminum wheels. The XJS line comprised four models, with 4.0-liter 6-cylinder and 6.0-liter V-12 engines in coupes and convertibles.

1996 XJ12
1996 was the last year for the XJ12 sedan. The V-12-engined variation of the X300 was powered by a 6.0-liter engine that was a derivation of the previous 5.3-liter version. With a longer stroke, power was increased as was mid-range torque. The bodyshell had been modified in 1992 to accommodate the V-12 engine, with about 60 of the 140 new or modified panels associated with the V-12 installation. While many of the panels were required for the V-12 engine installation, several were also necessitated by the installation of a driver's-side airbag, including the required chassis stiffening.

of $65,000, just $6,600 more than the base XJ6.

The sedan line was based on the Series III or X300 as it was known internally. The base engine for the sedans was the AJ16, a 4.0-liter inline six based on the AJ6. It developed 245 horsepower, a 10 percent increase over 1994. Exterior styling of the new sedans was smoother and more aerodynamic. As in previous years, grille design differentiated the models.

For 1996, long wheelbase versions of the X300 sedans were introduced. The X300 LWB sedans

rode on a 117.9-inch wheelbase, compared to the standard 113.0-inch wheelbase. In 1996, this chassis was used only for the Vanden Plas and XJ12, but in 1997, with the discontinuance of the V-12-engined car, it became available on XJ6L and Vanden Plas. A short wheelbase XJ6 remained in the line and the XJR kept the short wheelbase as well.

Nicholas Scheele joined Jaguar from Ford of Mexico in 1992 as Chairman and CEO, with the same commitment to quality improvement

1996 XJS

In its last full year of production, the 1996 XJS was offered only as a convertible and only with the 6.0-liter V-12 engine. Coincident with the discontinuance of the XJS, the V-12 engine was also discontinued. The engine of choice for Jaguar's new sports car would be a 4.0-liter V-8, the first V-8 in Jaguar's history. Still the XJs served a useful purpose in Jaguar's history. While not a pure sports car, it provided a continuation of Jaguar sports cars between the E-type and 1997 XK8.

as Hayden. Since taking office, he has pressed for further improvements, including the 21-day installation of a completely new "overhead" sedan assembly track at Browns Lane.

Ford has been relatively true to its initial promise to allow Jaguar to be Jaguar. When the purchase was announced, automotive analyst Maryann Keller said the buy-out was cheap for Ford, because it would have cost them more to develop their own line of luxury cars.

In December 1989, Jack Telnack, Ford vice president of design, told the International Motor Press Association that Ford's plans were to keep Jaguar's uniqueness. Although he also said, "There are so many things that can be done with the XJ6. The proportions are great and the car has a very distinctive silhouette. I would have killed to have that kind of tread and the cowl in that location and the low hood. And now it's right in our laps. We could . . . really clean it up and simplify it."

Chapter Eight | XK8

On the product side, Jaguar returned to the world of exciting sports cars in March and April 1996 with the introduction of the XK8 coupe and convertible, introduced at the Geneva and New York auto shows, respectively. They collected universal praise from all who saw and drove the cars. Nick Scheele said, "The XK8 reaffirms Jaguar's heritage of outstandingly beautiful sports cars. The dynamic style of the XK8 convertible and coupe can only begin to communicate the driving experience in store."

Powered by Jaguar's first V-8 engine, known as AJ-V8, the XK8's introduction meant the departure of its predecessor, the XJS. First intro-

The Jaguar XK8 has a wide oval grille that is reminiscent of the E-type. In addition, the modern halogen headlights offer greater candlepower than the sealed-beam headlights of the E-type, while returning to the classic fared in look of the past. The "power bulge" in the hood adds structural stiffness to the panel as well as a muscular look to the first new Jaguar sports car in 30 years.

duced in 1975, the XJS was Jaguar's best-selling sports car, with sales of approximately 112,000 units, and was in production longer than any other Jaguar, 21 years.

The AJ-V8 4.0-liter engine is a product of Jaguar's Whitley Engineering Centre in Coventry. It is only the fourth all-new engine designed by Jaguar. It is a four cam, 32-valve, 90-degree V-8 of 3,996 cc capacity that delivers 290 bhp at 6,100 rpm and 284 pounds feet torque at 4,250 rpm. Eighty percent of peak torque is available between 1,400 and 6,400 rpm. At its introduction, the engine represented best-in-class performance in a variety of measures, including specific power output, power density (engine weight versus power), powertrain rigidity and friction levels. Development of the AJ-V8 engine began in the mid-1980s with internal engineering studies that arose out of Jaguar's new-found independence from British Leyland. The first running prototype was produced in November 1991. The engine was benchmarked

JAGUAR XK8 COUPE

The 1997 Jaguar XK8 Coupe was introduced at the 1996 New York International Automobile Show to rave reviews. It is a classic aerodynamic design that harkens back to the original E-type of the 1960s with a wide oval grille, fared-in headlights and stunning lines. The XK8 is also powered by Jaguar's first V-8 engine, dubbed AJ-V8. It is only the fourth all-new engine designed by Jaguar. The car and engine were both designed in England. Design of the cars began in the early 1990s, but engine development began in the mid-1980s.

The smooth rear lines of the Jaguar XK8 Coupe hide a respectable 11.1 cubic foot trunk. In addition, there is carrying space behind the front seats. The two rear seats offer head and shoulder room that is only slightly less than that afforded to front seat passengers. The safety-mandated high-mounted stop light is mounted on the rear parcel shelf at the bottom of the windshield.

against the Lexus V-8 for refinement and the BMW V-8 for power delivery.

The square design of the AJ-V8 (86 mm bore x 86 mm stroke) was selected after considerable research with single-cylinder prototypes for its balance of power output with low emissions and high thermal efficiency.

While the 90-degree Vee angle is conventional and the all-aluminum construction is widespread, the die-cast block improves upon standard practice by employing a structural bedplate to establish a rigid, durable foundation for the engine. The bedplate is an intricate aluminum casting that forms the portion of the block below the crankshaft centerline, incorporating the five main bearing caps into a single ladder-type structure. Iron liners are cast in place at each bearing position to ensure that bearing clearance remains constant at all temperatures. Tying the bearing caps (which support the crankshaft) together with the bedplate results in a far stronger engine assembly that not only benefits long-term durability, but also helps to eliminate vibration at the source, improving refinement. It is a feature that is also employed in Cadillac's Northstar V-8 and the Oldsmobile Aurora V-8 that is derived from it and which, in highly modified form, will be one of two powerplants for Indy Racing League cars in 1997.

The working surface of the cylinder bores is formed by an electroplating process called Nikasil (for nickel/silicon carbide), which is applied directly to the aluminum parent material of the engine block. There are no separate iron cylinder liners. A precision casting of spheroidal graphite iron, the crankshaft has minimal bending and twisting under power.

With double overhead camshafts and four valves per cylinder, the AJ-V8 engine cylinder head continues a Jaguar tradition for advanced engine design. The head casting is produced through a proprietary technique developed by Cosworth. The engine's operating efficiency is aided by a narrow included valve angle of just 28 degrees between the intake and exhaust valves, which also contributes to the compact dimensions of the pent-roof combustion chamber.

Jaguar has designed variable cam phasing into the AJ-V8, which offers the midrange benefits of advanced cam timing and the high-speed advantage of retarded valve closing. The timing shift involves only the valve opening and closing points; it doesn't change the duration of the open period or the lift height to which the valve is opened.

Engine management electronics are supplied by Denso, formerly known as Nippondenso, and a company with considerable experience in the luxury market. Nippondenso supplied the management electronics for the 6.0-liter V-12.

Despite a considerable amount of available power, the XK8 does not have a gas guzzler penalty, as the V12 XJS it replaced did.

The all-aluminum AJ-V8 engine is coupled to Jaguar's first five-speed automatic transmission, manufactured by ZF. A unique feature is that the transmission fluid is installed at the factory and never needs to be checked by the owner.

There are two driver-selectable shift modes, Normal and Sport. Switching into Sport makes available a performance-oriented shift program, timing the gear changes for peak response. The transmission also carries a self-regulating "adaptive" feature, which enables it to compensate automatically for the effects of aging and to adjust shift quality based on slippage detected in actual use.

Jaguar's unique "J-gate" selector system is incorporated as well. The driver can operate the transmission in full automatic, or can manually shift between second, third and fourth gears, using the left side of the J-gate.

Front suspension of the XK8 incorporates a short- and long-arm double wishbone system. This style of suspension offers more vertical wheel travel and a greater potential for maximizing tire tread contact with the road. The front suspension is mounted to an aluminum cross-beam casting, which also supports the engine mounts. The use of a cross beam helps prevent noise and vibration generated at the road surface from being transmitted into the engine compartment.

Rear suspension is similar to that used in the XJR sedan. Like the front suspension, it uses a control arm design with coil springs and shock absorber mounted in a single unit. The spring is seated directly on the cast iron transverse lower wishbone, not the shock, which reduces friction to improve ride comfort and noise isolation.

Four-wheel disc brakes are used with a Teves Mk 20 anti-lock braking system. This Teves unit uses an Electronic Control Unit and four wheel-speed sensors. Brakes are 305 mm diameter at all four wheels and are also ventilated at all four wheels to improve resistance to fade and improve wet-weather performance.

The XK8 was designed at the Whitley Engineering Centre under Jaguar Styling Director Geoff Lawson. "One of the key factors in our choice of the coupe design was its ability to translate into a convertible," Lawson said. The fully lined and insulated convertible top retracts to a position slightly above the rear sheetmetal, and can be covered by an easily attached soft cover. Lawson added that, "A design that provides some soft material sitting proud of the sheetmetal is a cue of classic British coachwork. To stow the top under a hard panel would have required raising the rear sheetmetal, a measure not acceptable to us."

"With one-button operation and automatic latching, the XK8's top operation is among the

JAGUAR XK8 ROADSTER
In 1996, Jaguar introduced its first all-new sports car in 30 years, the XK8. The Roadster version exhibits clean aerodynamic lines combined with touches reminiscent of the E-type—wide oval grille, long nose and short tail, and striking performance. What the XK8 offers that the E-type didn't is greater attention to quality and the backing of the Ford Motor Company in the development of the car.

Like the classic British sports cars of the past, the XK8 Roadster's top does not retract completely into the rear deck when it is lowered. Rather, it is covered by a tonneau and is raised slightly above the body, lending a classic touch to this thoroughly modern sports car. Modern safety legislation also requires a high-mounted stop lamp, which is molded nicely into the rear deck lid just under the top. And unlike the classic sports cars of the past, the XK8 does not offer wire wheels as an option. The standard wheels are cast aluminum five-spoke units.

world's best," said chief program engineer Bob Dover. One of the salient features of the XK8 convertible is its fully lined top. Mohair lining and insulation give the XK8 the look and feel of a coupe with the top raised. On the highway at speeds up to 100 miles per hour, there is no wind noise. In fact, the XK8 convertible is in the same class as the famed Lexus LS400 as a quiet-running highway car.

Concept sketches for the XK8 began in 1991. Clay model construction began in January 1992. The final design theme was selected in October 1992.

Wood trim highlights the dash, as in Jaguars of old, and white-on-black analog instruments transmit information to the driver.

Jaguar is marketing the XK8 against the Mercedes-Benz SL500 and BMW 840Ci, and holds a price advantage of approximately $20,000 and $5,000 over those cars, respectively, based on 1997 pricing. The XK8 is still about $12,000 cheaper than the XJS it replaced, when you add in the XJS's $3,700 gas guzzler tax. Advertising debuted on October 3, 1996, with the theme, "A new breed of Jaguar."

As Jaguar cars have been modernized in construction and equipment, they have never lost their traditional looks and performance. Always built with the finest components and unsurpassed luxury, Jaguar products remain the equal of anything on the road in terms of speed, handling and safety. Through Ford's investments in manufacturing facilities and processes, the cars have reached a quality level which firmly ensures that Jaguar's reputation for value will carry on into the next century.

Bibliography

The literature about Jaguar is continually expanding. The books listed below were, in most cases, primary reference sources. Some are included because they are important general reference works for anyone interested in a more in-depth history of the company. Check your Motorbooks International catalog for any recent entries.

Essential Jaguar XK: XK120/140/150. Lawrence, Mike. Bay View Books, 1995.

Jaguar E-Type. Stone, Matthew L. Motorbooks International, 1995.

Jaguar E-Type: The definitive history. Porter, Philip. Automobile Quarterly, 1989.

Jaguar in America. Dugdale, John. Britbooks, 1993.

Jaguar Product Guide. CDI, 1995, 1996, 1997.

Jaguar, Fifth Edition. Lord Montagu of Beaulieu. Quiller Press, 1986.

Jaguar: Catalogue Raisonné 1922–1992. Automobilia, 1991.

Jaguar: History of a classic marque. Porter, Philip. Orion Books, 1988.

Jaguar: The history of a great British car. Whyte, Andrew. Patrick Stephens, Ltd., 1980.

Index